Educat

MW01482817

The Journal of the John Dewey Society
for the Study of Education and Culture

Education and Culture, published twice yearly by Purdue University Press, takes an integrated view of philosophical, historical, and sociological issues in education. Submissions of Dewey scholarship, as well as work inspired by Dewey's many interests, are welcome. JDS members receive the journal as part of their membership in the society.

Education and Culture is supported by the Daniel Tanner Foundation.

ISSN 1085-4908 (print)
ISSN 1559-1786 (online)
ISBN 978-1-55753-886-4

Submission Guidelines

E&C publishes critical essays, research studies, essay and book reviews, and commentaries to published pieces. Recommended lengths vary for critical essays, research studies, or essay reviews (7500 words); book reviews (1000–2000 words); and commentaries to published pieces (800 words).

Submit manuscripts to the journal's website:
http://docs.lib.purdue.edu/eandc/

Manuscripts should conform to the *Chicago Manual of Style,* and include a full bibliography and short notes. There should be no author identifiers in the manuscript file, as the review process is anonymous. Most editorial decisions are rendered within four months. Prospective authors are encouraged to contact the editor (granger@geneseo.edu) with any questions.

Send review copies of relevant books to:

Gonzalo A. Obelleiro
Instructional Assistant Professor of
Curriculum Studies, College of Education,
DePaul University
2247 N. Halsted
Chicago, IL 60614, Office #352

or

Eileen Susan Johnson
4820 Carrington Drive
Rochester, MI 48306
E-mail: johnso10@oakland.edu

Subscription Information

Send inquiries to:

Purdue University Press
c/o Baker & Taylor Publisher Services
Phone: 1-800-247-6553
Fax: 1-419-281-6883
E-mail: orders@btpubservices.com

Education & Culture is indexed in Cabell's *Directory, Content Pages in Education, CSA Sociological Abstracts,* ERIC, and *The Philosopher's Index.*

ISSN 1085-4908 (print)
ISSN 1559-1786 (online)
ISBN 978-1-55753-886-4
Volume 35, number 1 (2019)

CONTENTS

Editor's Note

David Granger

Greetings, readers, and welcome to the spring 2019 issue of *Education & Culture*. This latest edition of the journal features four articles and two book reviews, and it should come as no surprise to anyone familiar with recent scholarship on Dewey that all of the contributors speak in some way to contemporary issues and problems related to the prospects for democracy and/in diversity.

We begin with Kathy Hytten's "Cultivating Democratic Hope in Dark Times: Strategies for Action." In her contribution, Hytten explores the necessity for a democratic conception of hope that might help us more effectively counter the many social, political, and educational challenges we face today. In doing so, she appeals to possibilities for "storying our present" as a means of cultivating such hope, along with strategies utilizing creativity, mindfulness, and community building. All of these agencies of hope, Hytten argues in Deweyan spirit, might be effectively cultivated in schools. Shane Ralston pursues a similar interest in democratic means for achieving democratic ends in "Dewey's Political Technology from an Anthropological Perspective." Here, Ralston argues that Dewey's relative silence regarding the development and implementation of political technology to pursue democratic ends is understandable when this technology is viewed from an anthropological perspective. Utilizing such a perspective, he argues, helps us to see and appreciate the "myriad social and cultural conditions" reflected in human experience, and thus why Dewey was likely worried that specifying explicit means for intelligent action in political matters might ultimately "stymie the organic development of political practice." This explains why Dewey often appealed very generally to "the means of education and growth" while intentionally leaving "the task of specifying exact political technology (or which democratic means are best suited to achieve democratic ends) unfinished."

In "Bordentown: Where Dewey's 'Learning to Earn' Met Du Boisian Educational Priorities," Connie Goddard begins by reminding readers that both Dewey and Du Bois were strong critics of the narrow focus and concomitant limitations of traditional forms of vocational education. However, she proceeds to demonstrate how a careful review of the mission and accomplishments of the Bordentown Manual Training and Industrial School for Colored Youth (1886–1955) reveals that it largely managed to avoid these pitfalls. Unfortunately, Goddard notes, the school's legacy has been mostly ignored by historians, while Dewey and Du Bois apparently never had (or took) the opportunity to discuss substantively their intersecting views regarding vocational education or the Bordentown school. Our final article likewise looks to the application of Dewey's ideas at the school level. Sabrina Goldberg's "Dewey's Ideas in Action! Continuing Professional Development in an International Community of Practice" details the authors' experiences providing field-based teacher education and professional development during the 2017 EdTech Summit in South Africa. Goldberg's reflections make clear that communities of practice are no longer necessarily constrained by geographical locations and boundaries, but that information technology resources and training are necessary to reap the full benefits of long-distance communities. Addressing these issues effectively, she argues, often calls for Deweyan collaboration across differences and creative problem solving, especially in places where up-to-date information technologies and user skill sets currently are limited.

Two book reviews bring this issue of the journal to a close. The first is Catherine Willoughby's review of Charles F. Howlett and Audrey Cohan's compellingly argued *John Dewey, America's Peace-Minded Educator*. Our second book, Joseph Grange's wide-ranging *Comparative Assessment in John Dewey, Confucius, and Global Philosophy*, is thoughtfully reviewed by Holly Walker-Coté.

Enjoy!

—David Granger
State University of New York at Geneseo

CULTIVATING DEMOCRATIC HOPE IN DARK TIMES: STRATEGIES FOR ACTION

Kathy Hytten

ABSTRACT

In this essay, I reflect on the need for an activist notion of hope as an antidote to the social, political, and educational challenges we face in our current times. I first discuss some of these challenges as well as emergent signs of hope based upon different ways of telling the stories of our present. I then define hope as a way of being and intervening in the world, as opposed to a personal character trait or optimistic demeanor, and discuss some enemies of hope. In the heart of the essay, I discuss four important habits of hope that can be cultivated and taught in schools: storytelling, creativity, mindfulness, and community building. I end by discussing ways in which schools can help cultivate the kinds of democratic, critical, and activist forms of hope that can buoy and sustain us in dark times, as well as transform our world.

Over the past few decades, there has been a complicated and often paradoxical public dialogue around the idea of hope. While hope has always been called upon as part of the struggle for social justice and as a motivator and sustainer of work toward creating a better world; it is also something many see as fleeting and naïve, something that can actually get in the way of righteous indignation and revolutionary action. Hope has been discussed as a character trait, similar to grit, for example, as something that successful people possess.[1] It has also been described as a habit and way of being in the world that can be nurtured. Former President Obama's election campaigns were built around audacious hope,[2] and for a time, the excitement and energy of Obama's hope-fueled dreams for a better America were palpable, at least in some spheres. Yet for many, hope has fallen on dark times, especially democratic hope. Even worse, we have witnessed an active assault on hope, and concurrently democracy, especially in urban areas. This is evident in the lack of commitment to public goods, the overinvestment in a prison industrial complex, and the seeming celebration of shallow forms of hokey and mythical hope that are only loosely veiled covers for neoliberal exaltations of individual achievement and glory above all else.[3] Our current realities demand new forms of hope: democratic, pragmatist, critical, and ultimately activist. Cultivating democratic hope as a strategy for intervening in the world is an antidote to cynicism, passivism, and despair. It is also a strategy for combating pervasive polarization and helping to build bridges across lines of ideological difference. This is not a hope played out as naïve optimism or spectator-like cheerfulness, but it is grounded in everyday actions that can create different ways of being, interacting, healing, and transforming the world.

No doubt our current social, political, ecological, educational, and even interpersonal climate challenges our ability to be hopeful. We are now living in a world where, at least among those in power, there is a blatant disregard for truth and evidence, conspicuous attacks on the most vulnerable of our citizens, and a devaluing, if not outright dismissal, of all things public. I see the impact of our surreal current climate all around me. People are divided, and many are stressed, anxious, shocked, angry, and downright terrified. We are overwhelmed by the challenges ahead of us and many of us feel powerless to respond to what increasingly feels like fascism weighing down on us. And no doubt this weight falls differently upon our bodies, especially depending on our levels of privilege and economic and relational security. The stresses of our public sphere are omnipresent in schools, where students in our most impoverished areas are exhorted simply to work harder. Meanwhile, resources to support high quality education for all students are increasingly shifted toward private, for-profit educational businesses and into the hands of individuals, in the form of competitive voucher systems. These shifts ensure that we have winners and losers in the very system that has historically been set up to level hierarchies, not exacerbate them. It is certainly a cause for despair that public commitment and support of education, alongside other public goods, has been drastically eviscerated under our current political administration, even as this pattern was also present in previous, more progressive administrations. So too are mind-boggling acts of violence, including the repeated pattern of tragic mass shootings in U.S. schools.

At the same time, there are also signs of resistance and movement building all around us. For many, it is a kind of awakening. For example, by conservative estimates, over 4 million people marched around the United States and throughout the world the day after our most recent presidential inauguration, demanding not just women's rights, but rights and fair treatment for all marginalized citizens, including minorities, immigrants, refugees, indigenous people, the poor, and members of GLBTQ community. The guiding visions and principles of the women-led, yet intentionally inclusive, march included calls for racial justice; an end to police brutality and racial profiling; reproductive freedom; universal access to non-judgmental comprehensive healthcare benefits; equitable opportunities in education, employment, and housing; transparency in the economy; equal pay for equal work; a living minimum wage; and protection of natural resources and the environment.[4] More recently, high school students led a massive march on Washington (supported by concurrent marches and rallies around the world) to call for stricter gun control laws. Teachers have led strikes and walkouts recently in West

Virginia, Kentucky, Oklahoma, Arizona, Colorado, and North Carolina. These large-scale movements and protests add to a long history of citizens speaking back to oppression, as evident most recently in the Occupy Movement, Black Lives Matter, and in the Forward Together Moral Movement in North Carolina, which has entailed myriad daily forms of direct action, protest, and resistance for over a decade. How we tell the story of current events, and what democratic activism and resistance has looked like historically, matters.

My goal in this essay is to offer both provocations and inspiration, democratic "hopefulness" about our present, and concrete ways to cultivate strategies for building and sustaining hope that can sustain us in dark and polarized times. I qualify the kind of hope I am describing as "democratic" and discuss the vision of democracy that supports this hopefulness. I also describe actions we can take in both the public sphere and as educators to sustain hopefulness. These actions can support students in becoming social justice-oriented citizens who are committed to democratic public goods and who are disposed to work with others, especially across lines of difference, to build a better world. The idea of strategies for hope is important. As I argue, hope is embedded in actions, it is way of being in the world, not a personal demeanor or individual character trait.

I begin by reflecting on some of the challenges we face that call for new and renewed ways of embodying democratic hope, as well as pointing out some of the enemies of hope. I then briefly discuss the emergent signs of democratic hope around us, along with different ways to tell the story our present. From there, I get into the heart of my essay, defining democratic hope and describing strategies to build and sustain this hope that can be cultivated and taught, including in schools. These build on some familiar democratic habits, such as persistence, resourcefulness, critical thinking, experimentation, attentiveness, trust, open-mindedness, and the like. However, they also involve more concrete actions that we can take in the present. I focus on four strategies: storytelling, creativity, mindfulness, and community building. I end by suggesting that creating and sustaining strategies of democratic hopefulness can buoy us in dark times and help us to persist in creating different realities. No doubt "we live in a contradictory world," writes Paul Loeb. "Dispiriting events coincide with progress for human dignity. But when change occurs, it is because people persist, whatever the nature of their causes."[5] While the times may be dark, nevertheless, people continually resist and persist in working toward more democratic realities. Adopting specific and ongoing strategies of hopeful action can help us make democratic hope a way of everyday life.

The Challenges Ahead: Why We Need Hope

For many, and especially for critical and progressive educators, it might seem strange to enumerate all the challenges we currently face that ignite the need for democratic hope, as there are so many that they can start to feel overwhelming.

It seems like every day there is a new reason to be fearful or angry; there are new decisions made at our highest level of government that call into question everything we thought we knew—and cherished—about democracy. For many of us, we are living in surreal times, marked by a climate of fear, the willful ignorance of history and the law, and an attack on researchers and the press, sustained by the accusation that scientists and journalists are the new enemies in our democratic society. While I don't want to overstate, and thus give more power to, some of the frightening changes we have seen over the past two and a half years of the current political administration, it is worth naming some of the concrete social and political issues we are facing—the battles ahead of us which directly influence how we educate our next generation. However, it is also important to keep in mind that many of these issues are not particularly new; they are part of a long pattern of prioritizing individuals and the economy over community and social goods. In some ways, they are the logical culmination of the fomenting of fear that is part and parcel of neoliberal ideology. As Sarah Stitzlein describes it, "the American tradition of rugged individualism and contemporary neoliberalism" has increasingly led to a distrust of both institutions and fellow citizens and created a world where individuals primarily see themselves as competitors (as opposed to part of a larger community) who "seek private gain, sometimes at the expense of others," and who are lost in personal consumption, "rather than interacting with other people to find pleasure or solve problems."[6]

What is most striking in our current era is the transparency of neoliberal patterns that have been in place for decades but have been often obscured under more progressive rhetoric. Our current administration is explicitly built upon a politics of fear and isolation, not on global goodwill or a desire for greater international cooperation or unity—in the face of threats against all of humanity: violence, poverty, racism, greed, terrorism, and environmental crises, for example. Always overtly and conspicuously positioning America as first has, not surprisingly, also positioned us as a bully in the international arena. At the time at which I am writing this, we have rolled back women's rights and reinstated the "global gag rule," which pretty much guarantees that millions of women will be denied access to healthcare and family planning information. We have begun constructing walls to keep immigrants out and banned refugees and many Muslims from entering the United States, even as federal court judges have declared the ban unconstitutional. We have forcefully separated immigrant and refugee families, criminalizing and imprisoning children along the way. These actions have ripple effects, further dividing people and contributing to increasing polarization and distrust among citizens.

The consequences of fear, mistrust, individualism, and polarization are frightening. While these consequences have been troubling and morally problematic for quite some time; under our current government regime, they have moved to the realm of the terrifying and surreal. For instance, it is becoming all too common to see amateur videos of white Americans engaging in xenophobic and racist tirades against minoritized people in public spaces. We are manufacturing fake terrorist attacks. We have recommitted to building pipelines that threaten the livelihoods and water sources of many of our poorest citizens. We have actively removed information about climate change from the State Department website and prohibited government employees from sharing scientifically supported information about our environment. We have witnessed the executive branch of government significantly overstepping its bounds, challenging longstanding faith in the judiciary and the American system of checks and balances. Naming the very real threats to democracy posed by the current regime, former Secretary of State Madeleine Albright describes how the president of the United States "has attacked the judiciary, ridiculed the media, defended torture, condoned police brutality, urged supporters to rough up hecklers . . . equated mere policy disagreements with treason, [and] . . . tried to undermine faith in America's electoral process."[7] While it is hard not to become morally outraged in the face of the abuses of our current regime, it is important not to simply attribute these to one person, political party, or worldview, as tempting as that sometimes is. The problems we are now seeing in such great relief are a product of the systematic breakdown of American society that transcends administrations and political parties. They are also deeply connected to elevating economic goals and priorities about human needs and goods.

While some might think it alarmist, it is becoming increasingly fair to suggest that actions of our current leaders represent, perhaps, the pinnacle of patterns set in motion decades ago that mirror some of the telling warning signs of the growth of fascism. Fascism is not simply an anachronistic term to name a dark period in our world history, claims Henry Giroux, "but a theoretical and political signpost for understanding how democracy can be subverted, if not destroyed."[8] As the ideology of neoliberalism has grown over the past several decades, especially in the implicit belief that profits for a few are more important than the health and livelihoods of all people, so too have contemporary versions of fascism. While Giroux warned about this growth over a decade ago during the Bush era, his list of "central tendencies of proto-fascism" is eerily prescient. These tendencies were also simmering close to the surface in the Obama years, despite his more progressive and unifying political rhetoric. First, there is a culture of traditionalism and reactionary modernism, where women, immigrants, and minorities "know their place," the government serves the interests of the elite, political institutions are controlled by narrow interests, and there is a return to some presumed mystical past harmony. Second, there is the privatization and the corporatization of civil society and the "diminishment of public space."[9] Third, there is the creation of a culture of fear and "patriotic correctness designed to bolster a rampant nationalism and selective popularism."[10] Fourth, there is an effort to control the media, through regulation, consolidation, or what we are most witnessing now, "sympathetic media moguls and spokespeople."[11] Fifth, there is the manipulation of discourse, and the "rise of an Orwellian version of Newspeak,"[12] where we are asked not to trust the overwhelming weight of evidence, but what our leaders tell us is the truth. The idea of "alternative facts" coined by one of our presidential advisors to defend the crowd size at his inauguration might as well have come right out of Orwell's *1984*. Giroux adds other warning signs, such as an erosion of the separation between church and state, and growing militarization at home and abroad. Scarily, these warning signs sound a lot like a checklist for our current era. While it is perhaps easier now more than ever to see how these warnings are manifest in contemporary practices, they have been growing for many decades, not simply over the past two years.

Alongside these challenges come enemies of democratic hope: behaviors, attitudes, and habits that support problematic elements of the new status quo and fuel the growth of contemporary forms of fascism. David Halpin suggests that among these enemies are cynicism, which often seems fashionable these days; fatalism, which leads to a belief that resistance is futile; fundamentalism, which inspires calls for an almost evangelical adherence to tradition; and postmodern forms of relativism, which leave us struggling for any ethical anchors to ground our visions of a better world.[13] To these, Howard Zinn adds pessimism, which "becomes a self-fulfilling prophesy . . . [that] reproduces itself by crippling our willingness to act."[14] I add isolation from communities of support, vacuous distraction (including addictions to popular culture, social media, and electronic devices), reductive thinking (you are either with us on our terms or you support the status quo), and in-fighting among potential allies as enemies of hope. These culminate in one of the most profound contemporary enemies of hope: extreme polarization among our citizens, which compromises, if not destroys, our ability to work together on problems that impact all of us as citizens whose fates on this planet are inherently intermingled.

In the sphere of education, Jeffrey Duncan-Andrade identifies hokey hope, mythical hope, and hope deferred as additional enemies of hope.[15] Hokey hope is a call for an individualistic, pull yourself up from the bootstraps kind of hope that ignores the reality of systemic inequity and structural violence. Mythical hope is embedded in the false, ahistorical narrative of equal opportunity in our society, which has been employed routinely to conceal structural inequities. And hope deferred involves critique without a vision for transformative action. In contrast, fortunately there are other more galvanizing and enabling ways of understanding the meaning and power of hope and its relationship to action, activism, and social change. This is hope qualified by such terms as critical, democratic, pragmatist, defiant, resistant, audacious, bold, and collective. And there are signs of this kind of hope all around us too.

SIGNS OF HOPE

You don't have to look far to see visions of hope. People are organizing, resisting, protesting, and speaking truth to power. In some ways, these are signs that our democracy is working, as people realize they indeed have agency and that the world is what people make of it through their everyday choices. Reality is not simply given. There are growing national and international movements to, broadly speaking, sustain the promises of democracy and to make sure our government works for all citizens, not just the privileged elite. These movements are testament to the fact that people know the world is unfinished; that more and more us are taking active responsibility for shaping the future in directions different from the present. Democratic hopefulness is evident in a number of different contemporary movements: the March on Washington in support of gun control, the sit-ins at Standing Rock that halted the development of the Dakota Access Pipeline, Black Lives Matters protests against police brutality, opt-outs and walk-outs to defend public education, the Idle No More movement against the exploitation of natural resources, the DREAMers fighting for immigrant rights, and the Forward Together Moral Movement and annual Moral Marches in North Carolina.

If we pay attention, we will likely see much happening in our local communities that can help us to build and sustain democratic hope. There are meetings almost every night of people acting to bring about a better world: teach-ins, direct action trainings, movie and book clubs, letter-writing campaigns, open-mics, and creative gatherings of all kinds. As just a few examples, there is a growing "Indivisible" movement of people working nationally but uniting locally to fight back against a neoliberal agenda. They identify justice-oriented movements and actions for people to participate in regularly (https://www.indivisibleguide.com/about-us/). Local affiliates of "Solidarity Sundays," groups of progressive, feminist, anti-racist activists all over the country committed to resisting the abuses of our current regime and building a more just, peaceful, and equitable world, meet once a month to strategize and take actions together in shared spaces (https://www.solidaritysundays.org/). Organizations like the Wall-of-Us send out a list of weekly actions that citizens can take in their own communities as part a broader mission to "make it simply irresistible for Americans to become active participants in our democracy" (https://www.wall-of-us.org). Participants in these groups write letters and emails, make phone calls, share action strategies, and otherwise engage elected officials, all the while building organized activist communities that, at their best, transcend political affiliations and bring people together to identify and address issues important to all of us.

One positive side effect of growing frustration and despair is that it has also fomented democratic movement building, and a more visible hunger for deeper meaning and connection among people. Research also shows that many citizens, and especially the younger generation, are dismayed by polarizing politics and want leaders who engage in thoughtful, civil dialogue, and work towards collaboration, compromise, consensus, and common goods.[16] This is in stark contrast to a politics of winners and losers. This hunger and momentum can ideally fuel the development of longer-lasting coalitions across lines of difference. How we tell the stories of these movements matters, as does how we define democratic hope, and model and teach strategies of hopefulness.

What is Democratic Hope?

My central argument in this essay is that hope matters, and that we ought to cultivate and nourish democratic forms of hope. Yet I also realize that hope can mean many things, and unfortunately, is often reduced to simply a personal temperament or character trait, a foolishly naïve or romantic form of wishful thinking, or most recently, an engaging campaign slogan that now unfortunately rings a bit hollow. In defining hope, it is important to begin by differentiating it from optimism, a frequently invoked descriptor that does not get us very far, offering perhaps some inspiration but no vision or direction for how we ought to be in the world. Cornel West argues that "optimism adopts the role of the spectator who surveys the evidence in order to infer things are going to get better. . . . [Alternatively] hope enacts the stance of the participant who actively struggles" against challenges in front of them, creating new possibilities while working for the good, the just, and the moral.[17] Hope is a way of being in the world that compels us to act with intention, to occupy the here and now in ways that prefigure the world we envision. That is, hope is a "way of living prospectively in and engaging purposefully with the past and the present"[18] as part of shaping the future. It requires us to eschew complacency and to instead reflect critically on current circumstances, identify problems, seek "inclusive input on those problems," and envision and implement solutions.[19] It requires that we learn habits of thoughtfully engaging others who may disagree with our perspectives and work to find potential common grounds. Democratic hope involves an activist sense of making choices in the present so as to bring about the kind of future we imagine, specifically one marked by democratic social arrangements.

The kind of hope that I am calling for here is pragmatist, activist, justice-oriented, and ultimately, democratic. The vision of democracy I draw from in this essay is both Deweyan and critical. Dewey argues that democracy is more than just a form of government, it is a way of life that involves the collaborative interdependence of people who work together to solve problems and to create opportunities for all people to live rich and meaningful lives and to achieve their potential. From a critical perspective, it involves not just the quest for individual freedom but also a commitment to common goods, the welfare of fellow citizens, diversity, and the ethical and respectful treatment of all people. It is grounded in a vision of social justice, where cooperation is prized above competition, marginalization and inequity are challenged, and citizens have "a disposition towards social responsibility and civic engagement."[20] James Beane describes a social justice-oriented vision of democracy well. He argues that in a truly democratic society, all people would "be free from oppression and experience equitable treatment." Moreover, they would feel obliged to participate in our society, be informed about the world around them, make decisions based on evidence, promote equity, and "act in ways that generally enhance the social, political, and economic life of the larger society."[21]

One of the unique features of democratic, pragmatist hopefulness is that it involves learning from others and truly listening and attending to diverse perspectives. Dewey calls for the importance of open-mindedness, something that cannot readily develop when we dwell only in ideological enclaves and among people who think like us. He writes that such open-mindedness "includes an active desire to listen to more sides than one; to give heed to facts from whatever source they come; to give full attention to alternative possibilities; to recognize the possibility of error even in the beliefs that are dearest to us."[22] Naoko Saito suggests that open-mindedness is one of the three "ethical modes of relation to others" that is an important part of pragmatic hopefulness, alongside friendship and sympathy.[23] Friendship and sympathy are related. When we see others as part of larger communities of care, we are more likely to work to understand their experiences and perspectives, and to work to find common interests and a shared sense of justice. Similarly, Steven Fesmire argues that democratic hope is connected to thinking beyond "righteous certainty" and "habituated assumptions," and instead requires "public dialogue, social learning, restoration of trust, and reconciliation."[24] All of these entail working to find common ground and ways of working with diverse others to transform the world.

Democratic hope is best understood in active terms. Stitzlein suggests it is most "appropriate to think of hope as hoping—a verb, and ongoing activity."[25] Pragmatists connect hope with reflection, critical thinking, attentiveness, experimentation, and action. They also suggest it "is closely related to love, understood not in a romantic sense but as a passionate concern for some other's lives (that of one's children, one's neighbor, or someone who lives in a different part of our shared planet)—a transpersonal commitment to achieving a possible and preferred quality of future living that is not yet actual."[26] In this way, democratic hopefulness is an intentional practice of living conscientiously in community, always striving for a world that is more humane, just, and sustainable than the one we are living in now. Pragmatists describe hope "as intelligent action in relation to a desirable, though as-of-yet unachieved object or state of affairs."[27] At the heart of meaningful and intelligent action are habits, or dispositions, including ways of drawing on the best available information when making decisions, and "organizing our energies" so as to bring about successful actions.[28] Habits of pragmatic hopefulness include such behaviors as persistence, resourcefulness, courage, imagination, patience, self-control, humility, care, and flexibility. When we coordinate these habits, hope becomes more than a "passing feeling or attitude," but a "mode of character"[29]— a predisposition to combat pessimism and despair with action, and to find spaces to work with diverse others rather than simply attacking their ways of seeing.

Democratic, pragmatist hope is closely aligned with collective hope, which Shawn Ginwright defines as a social phenomenon, a form of resistance nurtured in communities; "a shared vision of what could be, with a shared commitment and determination to make it a reality."[30] Writing about the need for both hope and healing in urban schools, Ginwright argues that we should think about hope as more than just a psychological trait, but as something that should be developed and nurtured in institutions like schools, communities, and varied social networks. There are three key features to collective hope: shared experiences, social imagination, and critical action. First, shared experiences help us to develop a collective understanding about our social condition, including the challenges we face and the barriers we must confront in order to achieve equity and opportunity for all people. Second, social imagination entails constructing a vision of a more desirable future, one marked by freedom, peace, and justice. This is the kind of social justice-oriented, democratic vision that inspires many activist movements, outlined as part of the goals and platforms we are working to achieve. For example, the Forward Together Moral Movement in North Carolina offers what they call the people's agenda, which includes working for high-quality, well-funded, diverse public schools; livable wages; affordable housing; health care for all; support for Historically Black Colleges and Universities; immigrant rights; environmental justice; expansion and improvement of voter registration; public financing of elections; and reform of the criminal justice system.[31] Third, critical action occurs when people see the injustice around them as socially constructed and thus impermanent and changeable. When people act on identifiable goals, they develop a sense of "control over their future," as well as existential purpose and meaning.[32] These fuel democratic hope as a habit, an orientation, and a way of being that is contagious.

Hope and action are inextricably related and mutually reinforcing. As Rebecca Solnit writes, "if people find themselves living in a world in which some hopes are realized and some joys are incandescent and some boundaries between individual groups are lowered, even for an hour or a day or several months, that matters. Memory of joy and liberation can become a navigational tool, an identity, a gift."[33] It is when hopefulness becomes an everyday practice and when we routinely act in the present in ways that build toward the future we want, that we can best achieve our goals. One of these goals ought to be living more personally meaningful lives, marked by our "own better becoming through participating in a shared, intergenerationally effective agency in shaping a world that reflects our ideals."[34] To achieve our goals, we need to make hope an ongoing practice that is manifest in the ways in which we live our daily lives.

STRATEGIES FOR CULTIVATING DEMOCRATIC HOPE

If we believe in an activist notion of hope—as a verb, an activity, and a habit—one of the tasks ahead of us is to figure out how to best cultivate a coordinated set of actions and ways of being that support enduring democratic hopefulness. Many of us develop some of the more personal habits of hope, like perseverance, critical thinking, open-mindedness, and resourcefulness, in schools, and within our families and social networks. Yet we need more to sustain us in neoliberal times, and to create a more just, democratic future. Here I discuss four particularly valuable strategies or practices that can help us to develop and sustain democratic hope and provide examples of what they look like in practice and how they may be cultivated. These are strategies that both draw on our unique individual gifts, needs, and desires, but also put us in meaningful relationships with others as we "attempt to restore some semblance of grace, justice, and beauty to this world."[35] In this sense, they can help combat polarization and create communities marked by caring, respect, responsibility, and diversity. These strategies are storytelling, creativity, mindfulness, and community building. I do not suggest that any of these ideas are particularly novel, and indeed what I talk about in relation to each may sound familiar. Yet I think bringing them together and talking about them explicitly as a constellation of coordinated strategies that can be learned and cultivated, helps build a strong vision for what critical, democratic, activist hope can look like in the everyday.

Storytelling

A first important strategy for cultivating democratic hope involves learning how to tell the stories of activism and resistance, and of bi-partisan social change, in ways that are inspiring without being naïve, utopian, divisive, or defeatist. Too often we talk about uprisings, protests, and movements as if they come out of nowhere (as opposed to being the products of long histories of organizing), and then when they are over, or the movements fade away, we become cynical, lamenting when the goals we strove for are not fully or even mostly achieved. We are taught to think in simplistic, binary ways, as if we did not achieve complete success, then our efforts were futile, a distraction from the real work of "productive" citizenship. We also are taught to mock protest as a fool's errand, and to minimize both small and large-scale movements and actions, including even those that brought together many different people across many lines of difference while working for some common causes. The corporate owned media often creates or exacerbates this message of futility as well, downplaying or not even reporting on acts of resistance happening all around us. Yet how we story our past matters significantly. Howard Zinn argues that "to be hopeful in bad times is not just foolishly romantic," rather, it is based on understanding the myriad forms of compassion, courage, sacrifice, and kindness that have indeed changed the course of our history.[36] Civil disobedience and protests sometimes seem like rare, exceptional, "whirlwinds" of activity, but once you start looking for and studying them, "these once-in-a-lifetime uprisings start to appear constantly, in diverse forms and unexpected places."[37] Indeed, their regular existence historically around the world validates the frequent rallying cry of protesters that citizens speaking back to power "is what democracy looks like."

As a habit of hopefulness, we need to tell the stories of social movements differently, focusing at least in part on what has gone right, the shifts in consciousness we have achieved, the divides we have bridged, and the changes in policies and practices that mere decades ago would have seemed unimaginable. We also need to teach about social movements and their impacts. This hopeful practice of alternative storytelling is Rebecca Solnit's focus in *Hope in the Dark* and Paul Hawken's in *Blessed Unrest*. Solnit counters the despair felt by so many activists in the face of neoliberal greed and power consolidation with numerous stories of victories and achievements, reminding us that "profound change for the better does occur, even though it can be difficult to see because one of the most common effects of success is to be taken for granted."[38] Similarly, Hawken's goal in his book is to tell the story of what is "going right" around the world, offering narratives that engage both our hearts and minds, stories of "imagination and conviction, not defeatist accounts about the limits."[39] These defeatist stories become addictive, yet "inspiration is not garnered from the recitation of what is flawed; it resides, rather, in humanity's willingness to restore, redress, reform, rebuild, recover, reimagine, and reconsider."[40] As part of storying social movements differently, we also need to disrupt tendencies to be dismissive, especially of the efforts of potential allies when their strategies and tactics don't match our own. We need to build coalitions, particularly across lines of difference, and resist the temptation to belittle efforts that seem to have little immediate impact. Reducing the women's march to middle-class white women taking selfies with their clever signs only fuels defeatist narratives, when the energy provoked by that march instead can be harnessed and channeled into other potentially transformative outlets.

Creativity

A second powerful strategy of hopefulness is engaging in creative activity, particularly resistant and activist forms of art making and witnessing. Drawing on Dewey, Maxine Greene has long argued for the power of the arts in helping us to imagine the world as otherwise: more just, inclusive, and democratic. Creating and experiencing art fuels the social imagination and helps to nurture community across lines of difference. Greene argues that creative, artistic expression helps us to become more wide-awake in the world; "it lessens the social paralysis we see around us and restores the sense that something can be done in the name of what is decent and humane."[41] Engaging creatively can be cathartic, and artistic expression can help us to personally connect to, and humanize, issues that can feel overwhelming. Equally important, such creative expression can fuel democratic hope. Creative activity is one important outlet we have as humans for speaking back to the world around us: celebrating our joys, connecting our lives to those of others, expressing our outrage, illustrating our understanding, and asserting our existence and passions. Protest art, including things like street theater, puppetry, sign-making, rap cyphers, open-mics, flash mobs, political documentaries, revolutionary music and the like, all help to raise awareness and consciousness about issues, often through distilling key movement messages in memorable, catchy, and provocative ways. They are not distractions from the "real" work of social justice organizing; rather, they are essential to that work. Creative expression generates dialogue and brings "vitality and energy to advocacy," as "it reaches people at deeper emotional levels, conveying what cannot be said with mere facts."[42] That is, it engages people holistically, our hearts and minds, in ways that critical analysis alone typically cannot. Art offers a different kind of energy to democratic activism and can sometimes make the idea of activism feel less daunting and more inviting and soul nourishing. It can also help create openings to build community, see our fellow citizens more generously, defamiliarize what seems like common sense, and "move us toward a more empowered stance in the world."[43]

An equally important benefit of creative activity, especially when engaged in with others, is that it brings people together and helps to build communities of resistance, joy, and support. Here art can be a "tool for outreach" and a "catalyst for change," enabling people to build stronger relationships with their friends and neighbors (including those who initially might not seem likely allies), deepen their understanding of challenges, express their own personal connections to larger social and political issues, and discover how issues effect those around them, both near and far.[44] As a small example, I have gotten to know a number of my neighbors through artistic and creative expression, for instance, through gatherings organized by one of my neighbors on street corners and in backyards to paint wooden signs with messages of hope, community, and welcome that are spread throughout our part of town, displayed on many people's homes, steps, porches, and front yards. Creativity also brings joy and connection, both of which are necessary to sustain the hopeful habits of democratic citizenship over time. Moreover, creativity is also part of self-care and mindfulness, helping us to stay in touch with some of the most important parts of ourselves. Creative expression as part of participating in social movements reminds us that "we gain something profound when we stand up for our beliefs, just as part of us dies when we know that something is wrong but do nothing."[45] Paul Loeb suggests that we might call what we gain "radical dignity," maintaining that when we act, engage, and express "based on our conscience, we affirm our humanity—the core of who we are and what we hold in common with others."[46] Radical dignity also emerges as we practice various forms of mindfulness in our daily lives, both alone and with others.

Mindfulness

A third important strategy of democratic hopefulness is mindfulness. This can mean many things: meditating, reflecting, working to stay present with others, slowing down, unplugging, connecting with nature, cultivating a spiritual practice, breathing deeply, sharing, taking a walk, creating, caring for oneself and others, exercising, and turning off the news. One of the things that competitive, consumer oriented, neoliberal culture has fomented, especially (but not exclusively) within our current administration is a state of free-floating anxiety and feelings of perpetual outrage, in part as a response to the "perpetual chaos" and uncertainty that our leaders seem to generate on a daily, if not even hourly, basis.[47] Every time we look at the news or our social media accounts there seems to be some new tragedy or trauma, some constitutional violation, a new battle to fight, and even greater polarization. If we are not careful, we will quickly become exhausted and literally overwhelmed to the point where it effects our ability to function. While we cannot control the world around us, we can take ownership over how we react to challenges, starting where we are, and not trying to tackle all problems at once: "People who successfully cultivate hope in their everyday lives don't become paralyzed by seemingly insurmountable problems. They get involved. They do the good that they can, in the place where they are, with the tools and people around them. They find concrete and local opportunities to engage the work of redeeming our world."[48] People who are mindful work to lessen greed and hatred, while seeking wellbeing for themselves and others in their neighborhoods, communities, and throughout the world, all as part of working towards a Deweyan vision of creative democracy.[49] And in acting, even in small ways, we contribute to building the kind of society we want to live in, bringing to life our democratic visions, and creating what Myles Horton calls "islands of decency—little units that are contagious and can spread."[50]

One of the things that makes mindfulness practices so important to hope is the fact that they can be healing. Trauma, suffering, pain, and oppression all threaten our ability to be democratically hopeful. They deplete our energy, creativity, and resourcefulness and they close us off from meaningful relationships with others. Describing the challenges faced in many urban schools, which in many ways parallel the challenges we are facing as a nation, Ginwright argues that we need both hope and healing right now. Indeed, healing is in many ways a precondition for hope. He offers a framework of "healing justice" in education, which bridges healing and activist organizing, calling for strategies to disrupt injustice and oppression (e.g., born of racism, sexism, poverty, homophobia) and to address suffering, anxiety, fear, stress, and despair. Healing is thus a form of democratic political action, as individual wellbeing is necessary for successful organizing and social justice work. Healing justice involves transformative organizing, restorative justice, healing circles, and contemplative (mindfulness) practices, all with aims to restore, sustain, and expand health and wellbeing. Transformative organizing is a practice of mindfulness, built upon the idea "that social change is the result of individual and collective transformation of how we treat ourselves and relate to one another."[51] It involves reimagining ways to structure social, economic, political, educational, and judicial systems so they work for all people, while also becoming mindful about "how these structures influence our relationships, our values, and our behaviors."[52] Only when we practice mindfulness can we work collectively to confront injustice, building the communities of support and resistance that nurture and sustain hope, transcend polarization, and bring to fruition our most noble visions of democracy. Moreover, only when we are mindful can we temper moral outrage (directed at our leaders or at those who don't share our political beliefs) with collective action, moving from reactionary rage to activist community building.

Community Building

A fourth strategy of democratic hopefulness is community building. In order to successfully transform our worlds, we need to work in communion with others, expanding our sense of agency and collective power. Patrick Shade reminds us that "hoping is not a bootstraps operation but a practice of discovering, creating, or enhancing relationships whereby others are invested in our hopes and we in theirs."[53] Perhaps the biggest enemy of hope is isolation, which sadly is something so many of us feel all too often. One of the consequences of modernization and the growth of a culture of individualism, marked by excessive competition, private ownership, financial independence, and segregated living, is that we have grown more and more isolated from each other. In his recent book, *Tribe: On Homecoming and Belonging*, Sebastian Junger writes about why soldiers returning from war miss the battlefront, and why people in tribal societies had little concept of depression, because in both contexts, struggle gave people a sense of purpose, connection, and meaning. Similarly, he describes how natural disasters can bring people together in ways that very few other things in our life can, in part because they make everyone feel needed. Junger argues that "human beings need three basic things in order to be content: they need to feel competent at what they do; they need to feel authentic in their lives; and they need to feel connected to others."[54] Yet so many of us lack any meaningful connection to others; we simply are not needed: "the beauty and tragedy of the modern world is that it eliminates many situations that require people to demonstrate a commitment to the collective good."[55] We lack opportunities to develop genuine solidarity, even as we know interdependence and collective engagement (especially across lines of difference) are part of what it means to be human and are integral to sustaining democratic social relations.

Given how isolated so many people feel in our contemporary society, where genuine conversations are rare even when we are surrounded by others, working to build and nourish community is an especially important practice of hopefulness. In reflecting on why it is important to be politically active, Robert Jensen suggests we are most existentially alive when we are working towards something meaningful in community with others. Discussing organizing work, he writes that getting involved puts us in contact with "like-minded people. It sparks conversation. It creates space in which [we] . . . can think and feel . . . [our] way through difficult questions. . . . It provides the context for connections that go beyond superficial acquaintanceships. The joy is in the struggle, but not just because in struggle one connects to decent people."[56] Similarly, Sara Childers writes about the ways in which participating in the Women's March on Washington helped her to see and feel emerging solidarity. Reflecting back on her own experience, she writes, "I hold onto the labor and the love from the march, and I try to see allies where I once saw enemies. When I'm the only voice in the room, I expect that I am not alone."[57] Through engaging in mindful, creative activity with others, she was able to see potential for building bridges where in the past she only saw "us" and "them." Democratic hopefulness is fueled in community, where we see intimately how our own livelihoods are inextricably linked to the livelihoods of others. Building community require us to branch out of our comfort zones, invite others into our spaces, engage in the hard work of listening and collaborating, and recognize that success "requires ubiquity, a network of informants, a conspiracy of social imaginaries, groups that cultivate new knowledge."[58] It is not driven by individuals acting alone. Nothing damages hopefulness more than isolation.

In many ways, all of the strategies I have described support the building of democratic communities that can fuel and sustain hopefulness. Indeed, communities, and what Dewey calls democratic publics, emerge through telling stories, acting creatively with others, and being present and mindful in shared spaces, including schools. Amy Shuffelton describes the phenomena of democratic community building well in relation to the 2012 Chicago Teachers Strike, in which a diverse public of teachers, families, and community citizens came together to challenge top-down, corporate educational reforms and teacher-blaming historically pervasive in the city.[59] Similarly, in studying how teachers have remained hopeful amid the challenges of neoliberal educational reforms, Mark Stern and Amy Brown describe the therapeutic function of action and community engagement, and in particular, teacher activist groups.[60] These groups help participants to create different narratives about what is going right in schools, showing individual teachers that they are not alone in their efforts, even when they feel isolated within their own buildings. They help these teachers to become more creative risk takers whose activism is sustained by the support of others. Indeed, in interviewing activist teachers, Stern and Brown found that these teachers continue to take part in teacher activist groups despite their always busy schedules "because being active and finding community is what makes teaching in depressed times not only tolerable, but also what has kept love, caring, and hope alive and able to grow."[61] These communities cultivate and sustain the kinds of democratic hope that are needed in dark times. When we invite others into these communities, creating spaces for a diverse range of perspectives, we have the potential to truly build what Dewey so prized, which is a democratic society marked by amicable cooperation and "freer and more humane experience in which all share and to which all contribute."[62]

CULTIVATING HOPE: FINAL THOUGHTS AND EDUCATIONAL IMPLICATIONS

Taken together, when we weave different stories, tap into our creative potentials, act mindfully, and work to build democratic community, we shore up hopefulness as a way of being in the world, an orientation of the heart and mind, and as a habit of character. These strategies put us in contact with our fellow citizens whose fates are tied to ours, people who share visions of a more democratic world, and with whom we can build larger and larger "islands of decency."[63] One of the ironically hopeful aspects of our present condition is that things have gotten so bad, so borderline fascist that many people are waking up, becoming newly politicized, and resisting complacency. They are learning new ways to think about democracy and the role and responsibility of each individual in cultivating and sustaining it. That the frightening consequences of neoliberal competition, individualism, elitism, and polarization are coming to fruition may be precisely the catalyst that we need to galvanize action. Despite warning signs, the fact is that we just cannot predict the future. It is open and uncertain, and within that uncertainty there are always spaces to act, to influence, to advocate, and to make our voices heard. Our actions may not always have the impact that we desire, but it matters that we do them anyway. There is fulfillment, existential meaningfulness, and even joy in being involved with other people in working toward visions and ideals that are worth fighting for, and in living out those ideals in our everyday relationships. And, as Solnit reminds us, "joy is itself an insurrectionary force against the dreariness and dullness and isolation of everyday life."[64] In this sense, joy, engagement, and the building of community and solidarity are what can sustain our hope and resistance in dark times. Democratic hope is the product of the actions we take in our everyday lives, both the mundane and the grander in vision, and especially those actions that help us to see allies where we once only saw enemies.

While I don't have the space here to translate the strategies I have discussed into concrete educational practices, no doubt educational spaces are ideal locations for cultivating democratic hope. This is, in part, because they bring together people with a range of backgrounds and experiences where they can practice different ways of telling stories about our present, creatively naming and speaking back to challenges, engaging in mindfulness, and building communities across lines of difference. There are myriad possibilities for engaging in strategies that cultivate democratic hopefulness in schools. These possibilities are limited only by our imagination. Strategies of hopefulness are best cultivated alongside learning habits of cooperative, critical, and democratic thinking. At the very least, we need curricula that encourage exploration, problem identification, problem solving, and political engagement. We need to provide kids with spaces to work together and to work on issues and problems that matter to them, that are current, and that impact them and their families. We need to focus less on content mastery, individual achievement, and competition, and more on what it means to be a person inheriting this flawed and yet beautiful world we all share.

Students develop democratic hope when exposed to a curriculum of meaningfulness and when they attend schools where relationships among students, teachers, and school staff are nurtured and valued. We need to teach habits of creativity, cooperation, resourcefulness, deliberation, democratic decision making, justice-oriented citizenship,[65] and dissent.[66] Alongside these, we should teach skills in conflict resolution, nonviolent communication, civic and community engagement, media literacy, and ethical engagement with others.[67] As the editors of the progressive education journal *Rethinking Schools* assert, our responsibility to students and "to the future is to teach them what it means to be part of a loving community, part of a democracy. We need community meetings, talking circles, journaling, [and] visiting artists."[68] We need educational projects that bring students into the community and community members into schools. These skills and practices all contribute to building habits of being in the world that can nurture and sustain hopefulness. They remind us that the future is open and ours to shape in more just, ecological, interconnected, and loving ways than we are now witnessing.

Democratic hope is sometimes most present in surprising places, where suffering and injustice are all too common. We should not think in terms of searching to find hope, but rather in creating the conditions for it to grow and thrive, and for it to help bring diverse groups of people together to work for common goods. Greg Michie tells a powerful story about the most provocative and urgent question asked by one of his 8th grade students at the end of a difficult year, where they had lost classmates and family members to violence in their south side Chicago community, and where many of them, as children of immigrants, were terrified after the election and inauguration of a president who promised to enact laws and policies that could devastate their families and communities. The simple yet deeply philosophical question she asked was "how does hope unfold?"[69] She did not ask where we look for hope, or how we can find it, but how does it come to be, and implicitly, how can we contribute to its unfolding? As Michie writes, "the image it brings to mind . . . is of hope as a process, a series of actions, that build on one another over time." In his school, the way forward was to continue to cultivate practices and strategies of democratic hopefulness; to "trudge through the losses and pain hand in hand," building communities of solidarity and support, engaging in peace circles, participating in unity marches and rallies, and providing spaces to be mindful.[70] The creativity of a class of second graders, who delivered handmade cards and presents for his homeroom students to help console them and remind them to keep on living after their classmate was killed, is also a compelling testament to hope unfolding.

Ultimately, the more we engage with others in building the world we want to live in, and that we want to leave for our children, a world marked by social and economic justice and democratic relations, the greater the chance we have of developing strategies and practices of hopefulness that can be contagious. When popular discontent, resistance, and disobedience are "sufficiently widespread and prolonged," no oppressive regime can endure.[71] When we are democratically hopeful, we both know another world is possible, and we act to make it a reality. The words of Chimamanda Ngozi Adichie, the award-winning Nigerian novelist, are inspiring as we work to develop, sustain, and grow practices of hope, both in schools and in our everyday lives. In a recent *New Yorker* piece, she offers, "Now is the time to counter lies with facts, repeatedly and unflaggingly, while also proclaiming greater truths: of our equal humanity, of decency, of compassion. Every precious ideal must be reiterated, every obvious argument made, because an ugly idea left unchallenged begins to turn the color of normal. It does not have to be like this."[72] Building, nurturing, and maintaining strategies of democratic hopefulness in dark times ensures that atrocities in our current world never become normal. It helps us to channel outrage productively as we work to build communities across lines of difference. It also allows us to develop hope that is meaningful, motivating, and transformative. This is hope that bolsters and enriches, rather than diminishes, our fragile democracy.

Notes

1. Charity Anderson, Ashley C. Turner, Ryan D. Heath, and Charles M. Payne. "On the Meaning of Grit...and Hope...and Fate Control...and Alienation... and Locus of Control...and...Self-Efficacy...and...Effort Optimism...and...," *The Urban Review* 48, no. 2 (2016): 198–219, https://doi.org/10.1007/s11256-016-0351-3.

2. Barack Obama, *The Audacity of Hope: Thoughts on Reclaiming the American Dream* (New York: Random House, 2006).

3. Jeffrey M. R. Duncan-Andrade, "Note to Educators: Hope Required When Growing Roses in Concrete," *Harvard Educational Review* 79, no. 2 (2009): 181–94, https://doi.org/10.17763/haer.79.2.nu3436017730384w.

4. Women's March on Washington, Unity Principles, retrieved from: https://www.womensmarchglobal.org/about/unity-principles/

5. Paul R. Loeb, "Introduction," in *The Impossible Will Take a Little While: Perseverance and Hope in Troubled Times*, ed. Paul R. Loeb (New York: Basic Books, 2014), 8.

6. Sarah M. Stitzlein, *American Public Education and the Responsibility of its Citizens* (New York: Oxford University Press, 2017), 188.

7. Madeleine Albright, "Will We Stop Trump Before It's Too Late?" *New York Times, Sunday Review,* April 6, 2018, http://nyti.ms/2GFY3XO.

8. Henry A. Giroux. *The Terror of Neoliberalism: Authoritarianism and the Eclipse of Democracy* (Boulder: Paradigm Publishers, 2004), 14.

9. Giroux, 18.

10. Giroux, 19.

11. Giroux, 21.

12. Giroux, 23.

13. David Halpin, *Hope and Education: The Role of Utopian Imagination* (New York: Routledge Falmer, 2003), 18–21.

14. Howard Zinn. "The Optimism of Uncertainty," in *The Impossible Will Take a Little While: Perseverance and Hope in Troubled Times,* ed. Paul R. Loeb (New York: Basic Books, 2014), 85.

15. Duncan-Andrade, 182–85.

16. Stitzlein, 2017, 189.

17. Cornel West, "Prisoners of Hope," in *The Impossible Will Take a Little While: Perseverance and Hope in Troubled Times,* ed. Paul R. Loeb (New York: Basic Books, 2014), 346.

18. Halpin. 14–15.

19. Sarah M. Stitzlein. "Habits of Democracy: A Deweyan Approach to Citizenship Education in America Today," *Education and Culture* 30, no. 2 (2014): 77, https://doi.org/10.1353/eac.2014.0012.

20. Richard Neumann, "American Democracy at Risk," *Phi Delta Kappan* 89, no. 5 (2008): 332, https://doi.org/10.1177/003172170808900505.

21. James Beane, *A Reason to Teach* (Portsmouth: Heinemann, 2005), 9.

22. John Dewey, "How We Think," in *The Later Works of John Dewey, Vol. 8, 1925–1953: 1933, Essays and How We Think,* ed. Jo Ann Boydston (Carbondale, IL: Southern Illinois University Press, 1986), 136.

23. Naoko Saito, "Reconstruction in Dewey's Pragmatism: Home, Neighborhood, and Otherness," *Education and Culture* 25, no. 2 (2009): 102, https://docs.lib.purdue.edu/eandc/vol25/iss2/art10.

24. Steven Fesmire, "Democracy and the Industrial Imagination in American Education," *Education and Culture* 32, no. 1 (2016): 59, https://doi.org/10.5703/educationculture.32.1.53.

25. Sarah M. Stitzlein, *Teaching for Dissent: Citizenship Education and Political Activism* (Boulder: Paradigm Publishers, 2014), 149.

26. Judith M. Green, *Pragmatism and Social Hope: Deepening Democracy in Global Contexts* (New York: Columbia University Press, 2008), 102.

27. Carrie Nolan and Sarah M. Stitzlein, "Meaningful Hope for Teachers in Times of High Anxiety and Low Morale," *Democracy and Education* 19, no. 1 (2011): 3, https://democracyeducationjournal.org/home/vol19/iss1/2.

28. Patrick Shade, "Educating Hopes," *Studies in Philosophy and Education* 25, no. 3 (2006): 195, https://doi.org/10.1007/s11217-005-1251-2.

29. Shade, 197.

30. Shawn Ginwright, *Hope and Healing in Urban Education: How Urban Activists and teachers are Reclaiming Matters of the Heart* (New York: Routledge, 2016), 21.

31. Forward Together Moral Movement & HKONJ People's Assembly Coalition, People's Agenda, https://naacpnc.org/the-14-point-peoples-agenda.

32. Ginwright, *Hope and Healing in Urban Education*, 23–24.

33. Rebecca Solnit, *Hope in the Dark: Untold Histories, Wild Possibilities, 3rd Edition* (Chicago: Haymarket Books, 2016), xxv.

34. Green, *Pragmatism and Social Hope*, 191.

35. Paul Hawken, *Blessed Unrest: How the Largest Social Movement in History is Restoring Grace, Justice, and Beauty to the World* (New York: Penguin Books, 2007), 4.

36. Zinn, "The Optimism of Uncertainty," 86.

37. Mark Engler and Paul Engler, *This Is an Uprising: How Nonviolent Revolt Is Shaping the Twenty-First Century* (New York: Nation Books, 2016), xvi.

38. Chris Bright, as cited in Solnit, *Hope in the Dark*, 109.

39. Hawken, *Blessed Unrest*, 4.

40. Ibid.

41. Maxine Greene, *Releasing the Imagination: Essays on Education, the Arts, and Social Change* (San Francisco: Jossey-Bass, 1995), 35.

42. Kevin Zeese and Margaret Flowers, "Creative Resistance: Why We Need to Incorporate Art into Our Activism," *Alternet*, March 7, 2014, http://www.alternet.org/activism/we-need-art-our-activism.

43. Wendy Kohli, "The Dialectical Imagination of Maxine Greene: Social Imagination as Critical Pedagogy," *Education and Culture* 32, no. 1 (2016): 18, https:/doi.org/10.5703/educationculture.32.1.15.

44. Kohli, 18.

45. Loeb, "Introduction," 15.

46. Ibid.

47. Arianna Huffington, "How to Get Out of the Cycle of Outrage in a Trump World," *The Huffington Post,* February 7, 2017, http://www.huffingtonpost.com/entry/how-to-get-out-of-the-cycle-of-outrage-in-a-trump-world_us_5899f342e4b0406131394b0f.

48. Robert Hardies, "Three Ways to Cultivate a Sense of Hope, Even When Times Seem Hopeless," *The Washington Post,* December 21, 2016, https://www.washingtonpost.com/news/acts-of-faith/wp/2016/12/21/three-ways-to-cultivate-a-sense-of-hope-even-when-times-seem-hopeless/?utm_term=.e7abd359aa65.

49. Kyle A. Greenwalt and Cuong H. Nguyen, "The Mindfulness Practice,

Aesthetic Experience, and Creative Democracy," *Education and Culture* 33, no. 2 (2017): 61, https://docs.lib.purdue.edu/eandc/vol33/iss2/art4.

50. Myles Horton, as cited in Eliot Wigginton, *Sometimes a Shining Moment: The Foxfire Experience, Twenty Years Teaching in a High School Classroom* (New York: Anchor Books, 1985), 319.

51. Ginwright, *Hope and Healing in Urban Education*, 29.

52. Ibid.

53. Shade, "Educating Hopes," 10.

54. Sebastian Junger, *Tribe: On Homecoming and Belonging* (New York: Harper Collins, 2016), 22.

55. Junger, 59.

56. Robert Jensen, "Critical Hope: Radical Citizenship in Reactionary Times," *Common Dreams* (2001), 6, http://202.49.69.66/pma/rob00434.htm.

57. Sara M. Childers, "Commentary on the Women's March on Washington: How Does One become One Million?" *Educational Studies* 53, no. 3 (2017): 318, https://doi.org/10.1080/00131946.2017.1297303.

58. Hawken, *Blessed Unrest*, 178.

59. Amy B. Shuffelton, "The Chicago Teachers Strike and Its Public," *Education and Culture* 32, no. 2 (2014).

60. Mark Stern and Amy Brown, "'It's 5:30. I'm Exhausted. And I Have to Go All the Way to F*%#ing Fishtown.': Educator Depression, Activism, and Finding (Armed) Love in a Hopeless (Neoliberal) Place," *The Urban Review* 48, no. 2 (2016), https://doi.org/10.1007/s11256-016-0357-x.

61. Stern and Brown, 337.

62. John Dewey, "Creative Democracy – The Task Before Us," in *The Later Works of John Dewey, Vol. 14 1939–1941, Essays, Reviews, and Miscellany*, ed. Jo Ann Boydston, (Carbondale: Southern Illinois University Press, 1986), 230.

63. Horton, as cited in Wigginton, *Sometimes a Shining Moment*, 319.

64. Solnit, *Hope in the Dark*, xviii.

65. Joel Westheimer, *What Kind of Citizen?: Educating our Children for the Common Good* (New York: Teachers College Press, 2015).

66. Stitzlein, *Teaching for Dissent*.

67. H. Svi Shapiro, "Educating for Hope and Possibility in Troubled Times," *Tikkun Magazine*, 31, no. 4 (October 31, 2016).

68. Rethinking Schools, "In Our Hands," *Rethinking Schools* 31, no. 2 (2016–17): 5, https://www.rethinkingschools.org/articles/in-our-hands.

69. Greg Michie, "Unfolding Hope in a Chicago School," *Rethinking Schools* 31, no. 3 (2017): 31, https://www.rethinkingschools.org/articles/unfolding-hope-in-a-chicago-school.

70. Ibid.

71. Engler and Engler, *This is an Uprising*, 91.

72. Chimamanda N. Adichie, "Now is the Time to Talk about What We Are Actually Talking About," *The New Yorker*, December 2, 2016, http://www.new yorker.com/culture/cultural-comment/now-is-the-time-to-talk-about-what-we -are-actually-talking-about.

BIBLIOGRAPHY

Adichie, Chimamanda N. "Now is the Time to Talk about What We Are Actually Talking About." *The New Yorker,* December 2, 2016. http://www.newyorker .com/culture/cultural-comment/now-is-the-time-to-talk-about-what-we-are -actually-talking-about.

Albright, Madeleine. "Will We Stop Trump Before It's Too Late?" *New York Times, Sunday Review,* April 6, 2018. Available at: http://nyti.ms/2GFY3XO.

Anderson, Charity, Ashley C. Turner, Ryan D. Heath, and Charles M. Payne. "On the Meaning of Grit…and Hope…and Fate Control…and Alienation…and Locus of Control…and…Self-Efficacy…and…Effort Optimism…and…" *Urban Review* 48, no. 2 (2016): 198–219. https://doi.org/10.1007/s11256-016-0351-3.

Beane, James. *A Reason to Teach.* New Hampshire: Heinemann, 2005.

Childers, Sara M. "Commentary on the Women's March on Washington: How Does One Become One Million?" *Educational Studies* 53, no. 3 (2017): 315–18. https://doi.org/10.1080/00131946.2017.1297303.

Dewey, John. "Creative Democracy – The Task Before Us," in *The Later Works of John Dewey, Vol. 1, 1939–1941, Essays, Reviews, and Miscellany.* Carbondale, IL: Southern Illinois University Press, 1986.

— — —. "How We Think." in *The Later Works of John Dewey, Volume 8, 1925–1953: 1933, Essays and How We Think,* ed. Jo Ann Boydston (Carbondale, IL: Southern Illinois University Press, 1986): 105–352.

Duncan-Andrade, Jeffery M. R. "Note to Educators: Hope Required When Growing Roses in Concrete." *Harvard Educational Review* 79, no. 2 (2009): 181–94. https://doi.org/10.17763/haer.79.2.nu3436017730384w.

Engler, Mark and Paul Engler. *This is an Uprising: How Nonviolent Revolt is Shaping the Twenty-first Century.* New York: Nation Books, 2016.

Fesmire, Steven. "Democracy and the Industrial Imagination in American Education." *Education and Culture* 32, no. 1 (2016): 53–61. https://doi.org /10.5703/educationculture.32.1.53.

Forward Together Moral Movement & HKONJ People's Assembly Coalition, People's Agenda. https://naacpnc.org/the-14-point-peoples-agenda/

Ginwright, Shawn. *Hope and Healing in Urban Education: How Urban Activists and Teachers Are Reclaiming Matters of the Heart.* New York: Routledge, 2016.

Giroux, Henry A. *The Terror of Neoliberalism: Authoritarianism and the Eclipse of Democracy.* Boulder: Paradigm Publishers, 2014.

Green, Judith M. *Pragmatism and Social Hope: Deepening Democracy in Global Contexts*. New York: Columbia University Press, 2008.

Greene, Maxine. *Releasing the Imagination: Essays on Education, the Arts, and Social Change*. San Francisco: Jossey-Bass, 1995.

Greenwalt, Kyle A. and Cuong H. Nguyen. "The Mindfulness Practice, Aesthetic Experience, and Creative Democracy." *Education and Culture* 33, no. 2 (2017): 49–65.

Halpin, David. *Hope and Education: The Role of Utopian Imagination*. New York, NY: Routledge Falmer, 2003.

Hardies, Robert. "Three Ways to Cultivate a Sense of Hope, Even When Times Seem Hopeless." *The Washington Post,* December 21, 2016. https://www.washingtonpost.com/news/acts-of-faith/wp/2016/12/21/three-ways-to-cultivate-a-sense-of-hope-even-when-times-seem-hopeless/?utm_term=.e7abd359aa65.

Hawken, Paul. *Blessed Unrest: How the Largest Social Movement in History is Restoring Grace, Justice, and Beauty to the World*. New York: Penguin Books, 2007.

Huffington, Arianna. How to Get Out of the Cycle of Outrage in a Trump World. *The Huffington Post,* February 7, 2017. http://www.huffingtonpost.com/entry/how-to-get-out-of-the-cycle-of-outrage-in-a-trump-world_us_5899f342e4b0406131394b0f.

Jensen, Robert. Critical hope: Radical Citizenship in Reactionary Times. *Common Dreams* (2001). http://202.49.69.66/pma/rob00434.htm

Junger, Sebastian. *Tribe: On homecoming and belonging*. New York: Harper Collins, 2016.

Kohli, Wendy. "The Dialectical Imagination of Maxine Greene: Social Imagination as Critical Pedagogy." *Education and Culture* 32, no. 1 (2016): 15–24. https://doi.org/10.5703/educationculture.32.1.15.

Loeb, Paul R. "Introduction." In *The Impossible Will Take a Little While: Perseverance and Hope in Troubled Times*, edited by Paul R. Loeb, 1–17. New York: Basic Books, 2014.

Michie, Greg. "Unfolding Hope in a Chicago School." Rethinking Schools 31, no. 3 (2017): 28–31. https://www.rethinkingschools.org/articles/unfolding-hope-in-a-chicago-school.

Neumann, Richard. "American Democracy at Risk." *Phi Delta Kappan* 89, no. 5 (2008): 328–39. https://doi.org/10.1177/003172170808900505.

Nolan, Carrie and Sarah M. Stitzlein. "Meaningful Hope for Teachers in Times of High Anxiety and Low Morale." *Democracy and Education* 19, no 1 (2011): 1–10. https://democracyeducationjournal.org/home/vol19/iss1/2.

Obama, Barack. *The Audacity of Hope: Thoughts on Reclaiming the American Dream*. New York, NY: Random House, 2006.

Rethinking Schools. "In Our Hands." *Rethinking Schools* 31 no. 2 (2016–17): 4–6.

Saito, Naoko. "Reconstruction in Dewey's Pragmatism: Home, Neighborhood, and Otherness." *Education and Culture* 25, no. 2: 101–14. https://www.rethinkingschools.org/articles/in-our-hands.

Shade, Patrick. "Educating hopes." *Studies in Philosophy and Education* 25, no. 3 (2006): 191–225. https://doi.org/10.1007/s11217-005-1251-2.

Shapiro, H. Svi. Educating for Hope and Possibility in Troubled Times. *Tikkun Magazine* 31, no. 4 (October 31, 2016): 37–45.

Shuffelton, Amy B. "The Chicago Teachers Strike and Its Public." *Education and Culture* 32, no. 2 (2014): 21–33.

Solnit, Rebecca. *Hope in the Dark: Untold Histories, Wild Possibilities*. Chicago: Haymarket Books, 2016.

Stern, Mark and Amy Brown. "'It's 5:30. I'm Exhausted. And I have to Go All the Way to F*%#ing Fishtown.': Educator Depression, Activism, and Finding (Armed) Love in a Hopeless (Neoliberal) Place." *The Urban Review* 48, no. 2 (2016): 333–54. https://doi.org/10.1007/s11256-016-0357-x.

Stitzlein, Sarah M. *American Public Education and the Responsibility of its Citizens*. New York: Oxford University Press, 2017.

— — —. "Habits of Democracy: A Deweyan Approach to Citizenship Education in America Today." *Education and Culture* 30, no. 2 (2014): 61–86. https://doi.org/10.1353/eac.2014.0012.

— — —. *Teaching for Dissent: Citizenship Education and Political Activism*. Boulder, Colorado: Paradigm Publishers, 2014.

West, Cornel. "Prisoners of Hope." In *The Impossible Will Take a Little While: Perseverance and Hope in Troubled Times*, edited by Paul R. Loeb, 343–46. New York: Basic Books, 2014.

Westheimer, Joel. *What Kind of Citizen?: Educating our Children for the Common Good*. New York: Teachers College Press, 2015.

Wigginton, Eliot. *Sometimes a Shining Moment: The Foxfire Experience, Twenty Years Teaching in a High School Classroom*. New York, NY: Anchor Books, 1985.

Women's March on Washington, Unity Principles. https://womensmarchglobal.org/about/unity-principles.

Zeese, Kevin and Margaret Flowers. "Creative Resistance: Why We Need to Incorporate Art into our Activism." *Alternet,* March 7, 2014. http://www.alternet.org/activism/we-need-art-our-activism

Zinn, Howard. "The optimism of uncertainty." In *The Impossible Will Take a Little While: Perseverance and Hope in Troubled Times*, edited by Paul R. Loeb, 78–86. New York: Basic Books, 2014.

Kathy Hytten is a professor in the Educational Leadership and Cultural Foundations Department at the University of North Carolina at Greensboro.

DEWEY'S POLITICAL TECHNOLOGY FROM AN ANTHROPOLOGICAL PERSPECTIVE

Shane J. Ralston

ABSTRACT

This article explores the possibility that John Dewey's silence about which democratic means are needed to achieve democratic ends, while confusing, makes greater sense if we appreciate the notion of political technology from an anthropological perspective. Michael Eldridge relates the exchange between John Herman Randall, Jr. and Dewey in which Dewey concedes "that I have done little or nothing in this direction [of outlining what constitutes adequate political technology, but that] does not detract from my recognition that in the concrete the invention of such a technology is the heart of the problem of intelligent action in political matters." Dewey's concession could be interpreted as an admission that he was unqualified to identify political machinery or institutions suitable for realizing his vision of democracy as a way of life. Not being able to specify adequate means to achieve lofty democratic ends is not problematic, though, if we appreciate the roots of Dewey's work (especially *Human Nature and Conduct*) in the anthropological writings of Immanuel Kant and Franz Boas. Experience reflects a myriad of social and cultural conditions such that specifying explicit means to structure that experience risks stymieing the organic development of political practice. When pressured to operationalize political technology, Dewey chose the appropriately open-ended and, at times, frustratingly vague means of education and growth. In short, Dewey did not want his ambitious democratic vision to outstrip the possibilities of practice, so he left the task of specifying exact political technology (or which democratic means are best suited to achieve democratic ends) unfinished.

> I believe that education is the fundamental method of social progress and reform.
>
> —John Dewey[1]

> In the broadest sense, it [Dewey's experimentalism] is the experimentalism of the anthropologist, of the student of human institutions and cultures, impressed by the fundamental role of habit in men and societies and by the manner in which those habits are altered and changed.
>
> —John Herman Randall, Jr.[2]

This article explores the possibility that John Dewey's silence on the matter of which democratic means are needed to achieve democratic ends, while confusing, makes greater sense if we appreciate the notion of political technology from an anthropological perspective. The late Michael Eldridge related the exchange between John Herman Randall, Jr. and Dewey in which Dewey concedes "that I have done little or nothing in this direction [of outlining what constitutes adequate political technology, but that] does not detract from my recognition that in the concrete the invention of such a technology is the heart of the problem of intelligent action in political matters."[3]

Dewey's concession could be interpreted as an admission that he was unqualified to identify political machinery or institutions suitable for his vision of democracy as a way of life. Not being able to specify adequate means to achieve lofty democratic ends is not problematic though, if we appreciate the roots of Dewey's work (especially *Human Nature and Conduct*) in the anthropological writings of Immanuel Kant and Franz Boas. Experience reflects a myriad of social and cultural conditions such that specifying explicit means to structure that experience risks stymieing the organic development of political practice. When pressured to operationalize political technology, Dewey chose the appropriately open-ended—and, at times, frustratingly vague—means of education and growth. In short, he did not want his ambitious democratic vision to outstrip the possibilities of practice, so he left the task of specifying exact political technology (or which democratic means are best suited to achieve democratic ends) unfinished. The importance of addressing this issue arises from the fact that much of the secondary literature on Deweyan democracy misconstrues Dewey's vagueness about exact political technology as a weakness of his political philosophy, when it is—I argue—its strength.

This article is organized into four sections. In the first, I summarize Eldridge's treatment of Dewey's political technology as well as some work of his critics. These critics contend that either Dewey specified the wrong democratic means to achieve democratic ends or he was too agnostic about settling on what technology was required in advance of changing cultural and political conditions. The second section imagines that political technology is limited to institutions. Dewey's silence can then be interpreted as an attempt to maintain a sufficiently flexible institutional agenda. In the third section, it is argued that the institutionalist perspective proves incomplete and, therefore, needs to be supplemented with a more robust account. To this end, I propose that Dewey's failure to specify adequate political technology makes more sense if appreciated anthropologically, reflecting the importance Eldridge affords the notion of cultural instrumentalism and that Dewey, himself, gave to the concept of culture. The article concludes with some implications of my analysis for Dewey scholarship, generally, including a call for a closer study of the late Michael Eldridge's impressive scholarly work on Dewey's political technology, and grassroots political activism.

Dewey and the Problem of Political Technology

The essay "Democratic Ends Need Democratic Means for Their Realization" demonstrates how Dewey's conceptualization of the means-end relationship operates in a political context.[4] Originally Dewey presented it as an address to the Committee for Cultural Freedom at the outset of the Second World War and prior to U.S. involvement (1939, Germany had just invaded Poland). In the work, he expressed concern about the argument, prevalent among elites during the 1930s, that promoting democracy will at times require the use of non-democratic means or methods, such as violence, propaganda and torture, in order to secure democratic ends. Dewey noted that the problem of "repression of cultural freedom" in Germany, Japan and Italy cannot solely be due to their fascist political systems, but is symptomatic of defects in the wider culture. Likewise, he claimed that "our chief problems are those within our own culture."[5] He decried the use of undemocratic means (e.g., violence, totalitarian rule) for the sake of securing democratic ends. In other words, the ends do not always justify the means (despite the Jesuit maxim), and in fact noxious means can potentially poison perfectly acceptable ends. So, "resort to military force," he claims, is unjustified in promoting democracy. Instead, we should employ "democratic methods, methods of consultation, persuasion, negotiation, cooperative intelligence."[6] Moreover, the scope of democratic transformation should not be restricted to explicitly political arrangements, but ought to extend to "industry, education—or culture generally"—that is, to the whole of civil society.

Dewey's definition of democracy is alive with melioristic possibilities, or opportunities to unleash human potential. In the same year, but in a different address entitled "Creative Democracy—The Task before Us," he writes, "Democracy is a way of life controlled by a working faith in the possibilities of human nature."[7] If democracy cannot be attained by undemocratic means, then what means, methods and instruments are available to the democrat? What did Dewey mean by intelligent democratic methods? A short answer is technology that is adequate to achieve democratic ends.

Some possible candidates for what might count as adequate political technology are as follows:

1. Deliberative forums, such as town hall meetings and citizen assemblies;
2. Campaign finance reform or efforts to revise current laws that govern how money is contributed to and used by political action groups, political parties and candidates;
3. Transparent and accountable regulatory institutions or independent bodies that stop corruption and ensure proper checks and balances in a system of fair governance; and
4. Efforts to expand civic education and extend voting rights to marginalized or disempowered individuals and groups.

Dewey comes closest to advocating for the first candidate (and to a weaker extent the last three) in *The Public and Its Problems*. First, he distinguishes between political democracy and the social idea of democracy: "We have had occasion to refer in passing to the distinction between democracy as a social idea and political democracy as a system of government. The two are, of course, connected. The idea remains barren and empty save as it is incarnated in human relationships. Yet in discussion they may be distinguished."[8] Next, he defines political democracy as "those traditional political institutions" which include "general suffrage, elected representatives [and] majority rule."[9] Dewey connects the idea of representative democracy and the role of experts and government officials to political technology associated with citizen deliberation. Although Dewey never employs the term *deliberation* in the way deliberative democrats do today, he wields synonyms such as *inquiry*, *dialogue,* and *communication* to describe how citizens enrich democratic practice through discussion, not simply by voting in elections.[10] In *The Public and Its Problems*, he writes, "Systematic and continuous inquiry . . . and its results are but tools after all. Their final actuality is accomplished in face-to-face relationships by means of direct give and take. Logic in its fulfilment recurs to the primitive sense of the word: dialogue."[11] For Dewey, dialogue is the engine for democratic self-governance, the public ruling itself, since it ensures that government policies and actions may be criticized, petitioned, and eventually changed through citizen action. This, he insists, maximizes government accountability and minimizes the extent to which citizens will blindly follow state officials. Of course, Dewey acknowledges that officials are important, given their policy expertise and the daunting complexity of political problems. Ultimately, though, the idea of democracy should outstrip the state machinery, radiating into all aspects of life: "The idea of democracy is a wider and fuller idea than can be exemplified in the state at its best. To be realized it must affect all modes of human association, the family, the school, industry, religion."[12]

To make this point more clearly, Dewey abstains from dictating the requisite democratic technology in terms of specific political proposals, reforms, institutions, or practices. All we know is that adequate technology indicates political means that are properly adapted to the democratic end: namely, citizens realizing as fully as possible their individual and collective capacities ("the possibilities of human nature"). So, democratic transformation demands diligence and creativity, "the slow day by day adoption and contagious diffusion in every phase of our common life of methods that are identical with the ends to be reached."[13] Unfortunately, Dewey does not elaborate further.

Dewey's vagueness about the exact content of intelligent democratic means or political technology occupies Michael Eldridge's attention in chapter four of his book *Transforming Experience*. He turns to consider "the question of the adequacy of Dewey's political technology"—that is, whether the need for intelligent political practice is no more than an empty truism, given Dewey's silence about the requirements to realize it.[14] By failing to specify any requisite political competencies or institutions, Dewey was criticized by his younger colleague at Columbia University, John Herman Randall, Jr. In the essay "Dewey's Interpretation of the History of Philosophy," Randall quoted several passages of *Liberalism and Social Action* in which Dewey called for the reform of inherited institutional arrangements and their outmoded practices through the rigorous application of social intelligence. Institutional change was needed, but by what method could it be achieved? Of course, for Dewey, the method is predominantly educational. "Public agitation, propaganda, legislative and administrative action are effective in producing the change of disposition," Dewey wrote, "but only in the degree in which they are educative—that is to say, in the degree in which they modify mental and moral attitudes."[15] Randall did not criticize Dewey for turning the question of how to facilitate institutional change into the question of how to educate institutional change-makers. Rather, he challenged Dewey to identify the competencies that such a political education should aim to develop in citizens: "Instead of many fine generalities about the 'method of cooperative intelligence,' Dewey might well direct attention to the crucial problem of extending our political skill. For political skill can itself be taken as a technological problem to which inquiry can hope to bring an answer. . . . Thus by rights Dewey's philosophy should culminate in the earnest consideration of the social techniques for reorganizing beliefs and behaviours— techniques very different from those dealing with natural materials. It should issue in a social engineering, in an applied science of political education—and not merely in the hope that someday we may develop one."[16]

Dewey's response to Randall was diplomatic—almost to a fault. After thanking Randall for his careful critique, Dewey concedes that his democratic vision begs for more detail: "The fact—which he points out—that I have myself done little or nothing in this direction does not detract from my recognition that in the concrete the invention of such a technology is the heart of the problem of intelligent action in political matters."[17] Dewey's concession could be damning evidence that his political ideals were too lofty and his democratic dreams too utopic. Dewey distinguished political democracy, which signifies the institutional phase of democratic governance, and democracy as a social idea (or way of life), which points to the conceptual or theoretical phase.[18] Several contemporary commentators have criticized Dewey, similar to Randall, for failing to operationalize, or make concrete, the meaning of political democracy.[19]

Roger Ames suggests one reason for Dewey's silence. Specifying the requisite political skills and institutions for realizing democratic ends, besides being undemocratic, is potentially dangerous. Superficially democratic means can easily transform into conservative instruments of state sanctioned violence. Ames writes, "On Dewey's understanding, the familiar institutionalized forms of democracy—a constitution, the office of president, the polling station, the ballot box, and so on—far from being a guarantee of political order, can indeed become a source of just such coercion."[20] For instance, Dewey could have recommended a procedure for amending a state's constitution, one that is especially difficult to attain, on the rationale that it will sustain political order and continuity from one generation to the next. However, when the effect is to preserve a morally questionable constitutional provision (for instance, one that sustained practices of racial segregation), the constitutional provision converts to an undemocratic means or piece of political technology. Another problem with an individual (such as Dewey) determining what constitutes appropriate political technology in advance of democratic publics is that the resulting redefinition of genuine political culture prevents democratic growth. The ruling or elite culture becomes identical to political culture überhaupt, thereby foreclosing opportunities for social experimentation, popular criticism, and grassroots dissidence.[21] So, it appears that Dewey's move to demote political democracy relative to the aspirational ideal of democracy was warranted, given that the recommendation of absolute or fixed means is confining, tradition-bound, and potentially coercive.

While Ames offers one explanation for Dewey's silence on the matter of political technology, he does not tell us why Dewey would not postulate a set of intelligent political practices that, while tentatively democratic and fallible in light of future inquiries, could nevertheless inform political experiments aimed at achieving democratic ends. One approach, as we will be seen in the next section, is to describe Dewey as an institutionally oriented democratic theorist with an open-ended institutional agenda—that is, to appreciate Dewey's political technology, or lack thereof, from an institutionalist perspective.[22]

Another approach is to understand democratic means as culturally contingent and emergent phenomena, evoking similar notions in the work of Immanuel Kant and Franz Boas. I suggest that this approach works best if we appreciate Dewey's reasons for not specifying adequate political technology from an anthropological perspective.

FROM AN INSTITUTIONAL PERSPECTIVE

Institutions consist of funded beliefs and habits—what organizational theorists call *organizational culture*—the accretion of which have created objective organizations and agencies that persist in space and time.[23] According to Dewey, "[t]o say . . . [something] is institutionalized is to say that it involves a tough body of customs, ingrained habits of actions, organized and authorized standards, and methods of procedure."[24] So, ideas and ideals do not exhaust political experience; for their meaning to be suitably enriched, they should also manifest in stable political forms. However, ideals qualify the stability of institutional forms, permitting them to organically develop through critical scrutiny and reform.[25] While Dewey acknowledges that successful "institutions . . . are stable and enduring," their stability is "only relatively fixed" because "they constitute the structure of the processes that go on . . . and are not forced upon processes from without."[26] In Hegel's philosophy of right,[27] the dialectical opposition between intellect and sense gradually transforms into self-consciousness and social institutions from a raw physical world; ultimately, they are reconciled in the Absolute, where "the real is rational, and the rational is real." Although Dewey's Hegel-influenced pragmatism dispenses with the Absolute, it retains a concern for how ideas and ideals directly influence the growth of those habit-funded processes called institutions.[28]

An emphasis on institutions does not preclude a concern for individuals, though. Indeed, personal development is, for Dewey, a precondition for institutional development, for "individuals who are democratic in thought and action are the sole final warrant for the existence and endurance of democratic institutions."[29] So as not to pre-emptively foreclose the many possible avenues before us, Dewey purposely avoided recommending a set of institutional arrangements or a final destination in the quest to realize a better form of democracy. In stark contrast, Francis Fukuyama declares that, by the latter half of the twentieth-century, "the end point of mankind's ideological evolution and the universalization of Western liberal democracy as the final form of human government" had been reached. Rather than advocate for "political democracy" or a discrete set of political institutions (in Fukuyama's case, liberal democratic ones), Dewey proposed a set of leading principles or postulations that together are termed the "social idea" of democracy.[30] As postulations, these ideas are intended to direct subsequent investigations into the design of a stable and viable governing apparatus; however, taken alone, they have no direct correspondence with any particular set of institutions.[31]

Dewey understands democracy as an open-ended struggle to achieve an emancipatory ideal which enriches individual and communal experience. Although "the measure of the worth of any social institution" is usually its "limited and more immediately practical" consequences, what the measure should be, Dewey insists, is "its effect in enlarging and improving experience."[32] Realizing the ideal (i.e., the social idea of democracy) therefore requires institutional change. However, Dewey does not presume to know—let alone recommend—the content of that institutional change in advance of its determination by the people and institutions of actual political democracies (e.g., elections, commissions of inquiry, judicial decisions, and regulatory agency rulings). Generating social and political reforms demands institutional transformation. However, the instrumentalities of change should not be preordained by a philosopher. According to David Waddington, Dewey "refuse[d] to specify the shape of social change in advance. If social change is to be truly democratic, it needs to be placed in the hands of the demos, in the hands of the workers and citizens who will actually make the change."[33] Specifying the right political-institutional technology to obtain social change would block opportunities for citizens to develop competencies through their own participation in the process.

Whether eliminating apartheid in South Africa or ameliorating racial injustice in the Southern United States, change begs for experimentation with alternate institutions. James Campbell contends that pragmatist policy-making should resemble an open-ended experimental program: "[A]ll policy measures should be envisioned as experiments to be tested in their future consequences. As a consequence of this testing, the program will undergo ongoing revision."[34] Likewise, Dewey writes, "[t]hinking ends in experiment and experiment is an actual alteration of a physically antecedent situation in those details or respects which called for thought in order to do away with some evil [or problem]."[35] Given the experimental thrust of institutional makeovers, long-term consequences are often uncertain, even to those who initiate them. As Dewey observes, "the great social changes which have produced new social institutions have been the cumulative effect of flank movements that were not obvious at the time of their origin."[36] Likewise, pragmatist theorizing about political institutions could, either intentionally or inadvertently, contribute to these "flank movements" that beget institutional change.

Indeed, there is some circumstantial historical evidence for this, such as the immense influence Dewey and other classic American pragmatists' ideas had on the Progressive movement of the early twentieth-century; and, more recently, some of the language and concepts of contemporary pragmatism that seeped into Barack Obama's campaign for political change.[37] If they continue on this trajectory, it would appear that pragmatists might have their ideas and ideals realized in the design of new institutions and the reconstruction of old ones. Of course, there is also the risk that these pragmatist ideas and ideals will be diluted or distorted in the process of becoming institutionalized.[38]

Whatever the outcome of specific institutional recommendations, the marriage of institutionalism and pragmatism appears to resolve the political technology conundrum. From an institutionalist perspective, Dewey's silence on the matter of political technology is excusable. He was an institutionalist without a specific institutional agenda. He simply refused to specify the right institutional make-up in advance, so as not to foreclose opportunities for genuine experimentation and democratic choice.

From an Anthropological Perspective

When pragmatists become institutionalists, a closer association between political theory and practice is forged. However, the institutionalist perspective falls short of addressing the political technology problem for at least two reasons. One, Dewey still cannot respond to the objection that some set of experimental and fallible democratic means must be proposed if we are to have any hope of achieving democratic ends. As he famously declared, "[p]hilosophy recovers itself when it ceases to be a device for dealing with the problems of philosophers and becomes a method, cultivated by philosophers, for dealing with the problems of men."[39] Dewey's silence on the feasibility of particular institutional methods might be interpreted as a failure to address "the problems of men," an unwillingness to grapple with the practical obstacles institutional actors would face in implementing his vision of democracy. Two, democratic means are not exhausted by institutions, but extend downwards to even more tertiary tools and micro-level behaviors—specifically, to the political practices of agents who sometimes stand outside traditional institutional settings. For instance, political activists make demands on policymakers in ways that do not always involve formal petition, but extend to informal techniques, such as direct action and agitation. To call those techniques *institutions* would be a misnomer since the rationale for enacting them is that more traditional, institutionalized channels of redress have been exhausted. To deny political status to such activist techniques would be equally mistaken. If voice cannot be exercised in a traditional institutionalized setting, oftentimes the only alternative for the silenced or marginalized minority is to exit and resort to more radical means of political persuasion.

So, how do we understand Dewey's reluctance to specify exact political technology in a way that does not offend his concern with addressing the "problems of men" and accommodates the practices of political activists? A clue can be found in John Hermann Randall's comment that in "the broadest sense," Dewey's experimentalism "is the experimentalism of the anthropologist."[40] Late in life, Dewey expressed regret that he had not substituted the anthropological language of "culture" for "experience" in his landmark work *Experience and Nature* (1925):

> The name "culture" in its anthropological . . . sense designates the vast range of things experienced in an indefinite variety of ways. It possesses as a name just that body of substantial references which "experience" as a name has lost. It names artifacts which rank as "material" and operations upon and with material things. [. . .] "culture" designates, also in their reciprocal inter-connections, that immense diversity of human affairs, interests, concerns, values which compartmentalists pigeonhole under "religion," "aesthetics," "politics," "economics," etc., etc. Instead of separating, isolating, and insulating the many aspects of common life, "culture" holds them together in their human and humanistic unity—a service which "experience" has ceased to render."[41]

Dewey's preference for culture over experience signals not only a cultural turn in his writings, but also an anthropological turn. Culture is a more inclusive concept than experience, encompassing all those artifacts, ideas, and practices that make human life meaningful—including those conventionally bracketed under the headings "political" or "institutional." Taking an anthropological perspective is one way to sidestep the tendency among theorists to compartmentalize. To this end, I briefly examine the influence of Franz Boas 'and Immanuel Kant's anthropological writings on Dewey's views about culture, especially as they were expressed in *Human Nature and Conduct*, before returning to the main question of this inquiry:

How might we explain Dewey's silence about what constitutes adequate political technology without offending his concern with the "problems of men," and all the while accommodating the activities of political activists?

Franz Boas' and Dewey's tenures at Columbia University not only overlapped, but their correspondence reveals a degree of mutual intellectual influence beyond that of casual colleagues. In *The Mind of Primitive Man*, Boas dispelled the then-widespread presumption that racial differences were innate. Evidence suggested that these essentialized physical and cognitive differences reflected environmental and social differences instead.[42] Boas writes that "the variability in each racial unit is great. The almost insurmountable difficulty lies in the fact that physiological and psychological processes and particularly personality cannot be reduced to an absolute standard that is free of environmental elements. It is therefore gratuitous to claim that a race has a definite personality."[43] And elsewhere, he notes "that many so-called racial or hereditary traits are to be considered rather as a result of early exposure to certain forms of social conditions."[44] In a speech before the NAACP, Dewey would lean on Boas' findings in making his own argument against the view that racial differences are inherent.[45]

For Dewey and Boas, probably the most astounding area of intellectual confluence is their similar accounts of habits and the process of habituation. Boas writes, "The facts indicate that habits may modify structure . . . [which] suggests an instability of habits much greater than that of bodily form."[46] Human and non-human animals can overcome their hereditary limitations in the struggle to adapt to novel environmental conditions. The secret to adaptation is the development of new habits, which while more radical or unstable than an individual's morphology, can in time alter the habit-guided creature's bodily features. Where human behavior differs from non-human animal behavior is in the capacity to operate outside the range of "stereotyped" instincts, to engage in practice that "depends on local tradition and is learned."[47] In other words, habit formation in humans is tied to the perpetuation of culture, specifically the transference of traditions and localized knowledge through education. For Dewey, similar to Boas, what distinguishes humans from non-human animals is the capacity to develop intelligent habits and transmit cultural capital through the medium of education. According to Dewey, education is a "process of forming fundamental dispositions" or habits so that they "take effect in conduct."[48]

Besides the work of Boas, Dewey's views also found some inspiration in the anthropological writings of Immanuel Kant. Though Dewey was a regular critic of Kant (and his reading of Kant's work was distinctly Hegelian), his familiarity with Kant's opus is beyond question. Indeed, he wrote his lost doctoral dissertation on Kant's philosophical method and the problem of the external world.[49] In *Anthropology from a Pragmatic Point of View*, Kant considers the obstacles to rational self-management. In the first section (titled "Anthropological Didactic"), he addresses the psychological impediments, and in the second ("Anthropological Characteristic"), the physical and social hurdles to exercising reason in all areas of practical life.[50] Unlike Boas and Dewey, Kant propounded an essentialized theory of racial differences. He catalogued a list of these differences in the final part of the second section titled "The Character of the Species." To the book's credit, though, education factors feature strongly in the account of how humans rationally organize their individual and collective lives, controlling the will to act on their baser nature by becoming "educated to the good."[51] Unlike Dewey, Kant specifies exactly what political technology is required in order to attain this higher level of rational self-control. The recipe of political means for Kant is distinctly Republican: moral pedagogy, natural or non-dogmatic religion, and a civic constitution. With these instrumentalities, Kant believed that German culture could be brought into alignment with the dictates of reason and morality—or more plainly, with the requirements of Republican freedom. On at least the point that our notions of freedom, rationality and moral rightness are a function of culture, Dewey agreed with Kant.[52] For instance, in *Freedom and Culture* (1939), he writes that the "problem of freedom and of democratic institutions is tied up with the kind of culture that exists."[53]

However, Dewey disagreed with Kant that German culture would reach its zenith with the adoption of these three Republican political technologies. Earlier, in *German Philosophy and Politics*, Dewey accused Kant and German thinkers, generally, of advancing absolutist philosophies that deny the influence of culture, block the way toward social experimentation, and produce the conditions for statism and nationalism.[54] Likewise, as mentioned earlier, in "Democratic Ends Need Democratic Means for Their Realization" (1939), Dewey complained that the problem of "repression of cultural freedom" in Germany is not solely attributable to their fascist political system, but to their larger culture of absolutism, universalism, and strict obedience to a sense of moral duty at all costs.[55] While Dewey disputed whether Kant's recipe of political means (moral education, natural religion, and a civic constitution) had produced Republican freedom in Germany, he largely accepted Kant's argument in *Anthropology from a Pragmatic Point of View*. Large-scale political reforms demand similarly wide-ranging changes in a society's culture. Nevertheless, Dewey, unlike Kant, remained reluctant to specify what constitutes adequate political technology for realizing that change.

A further clue as to why Dewey was silent on the matter of political technology can be found in *Human Nature and Conduct* (1922), particularly in his treatment of habits. Dewey defines habit as "a way or manner of action, not a particular act or deed."[56] From a physiological perspective, habits resemble bodily functions, such as taking a breath or digesting food: "Breathing is an affair of the air as truly as of the lungs; digesting an affair of food as truly of tissues of the stomach."[57] From an ecological perspective, habits implicate more than an organism's body. Since a habit is a mode of conduct, not the conduct itself, habits also signify ways of adapting to an environment, not just the adaptations themselves. Habit-guided organism-environment interaction is not just a matter of an agent acting on a world, but of an organism behaving within and through a living system, executing its daily functions as part of a larger web of biotic relations. According to Tom Burke, the "basic picture, generally speaking, is that of a given organism/environment system performing a wide range of operations as a normal matter of course."[58] Whether within a simple biological system or complex social one, environmental disruptions stimulate efforts by organisms to restore equilibrium, to synchronize their (functionally defined) internal and external environments (what process biologist call 'homeostasis') and to subsequently adapt to environing conditions through habit-guided adjustments.

From an anthropological perspective, habitual conduct is social through and through, a matter of generating the proper conditions for intelligent political action. Dewey writes, "We must work on the environment not merely on the hearts of men. To think otherwise is to suppose that flowers can be raised in a desert or motor cars run in a jungle. Both things can happen and without a miracle. But only by first changing the jungle and desert."[59] To generate genuine political change, reformers must raise popular consciousness about problems and proposed solutions. In Dewey's words, they need to "work . . . on the hearts of men." However, to ignite a virtuous cycle, they must do more than simply reform the technology of change (changing the furniture, so-to-speak); they also need to transform the cultural and environmental conditions under which intelligent habits take form ("changing the jungle and the desert"). Predetermining the content of that political change, or specifying the exact political technology in advance, cuts the chord between habits and action, modes of conduct and the conduct itself, generating the action or conduct but not the reformist impulse that delivers us to intelligent reformist habits again and again. Thus, education is one of the few forms of political technology Dewey goes to any significant length to elaborate, for it is itself an open-ended process of forming good inclinations to action, enriching cooperative experience, and transmitting ideas from one generation to the next. Rather than perfectly anticipate outcomes (whether in terms of political institutions or practices), education provides the environmental and cultural conditions for cultivating those habits that lead individuals to engage in collective action—now and later. One way to suss out this conclusion is by distinguishing between political technologies and habits.[60] However, I believe that this path is unproductive because, as mentioned, political institutions are funded habits, so that the distinction ultimately turns out to be one without a difference. Educating for political action is a perfectly Deweyan interpretation of what constitutes adequate political technology within a thriving democratic society.

Conclusion

To conclude, I would like to return to the late Michael Eldridge's perspective on the matter of Dewey's silence about political technology by first discussing his commentary on the work of Randy Shaw and, lastly, by stating why we should make a closer study of this important scholar's work.

Eldridge elaborated on why Dewey's notion of political technology encompasses political activism. In *Transforming Experience*, he turns to Randy Shaw's work *The Activist's Handbook* as a resource for expanding Dewey's conception of political technology and responding to John Herman Randall's critique. Shaw, a law student and low-income housing activist, describes his general approach to organizing in a Deweyan spirit.[61] In Eldridge's words, Shaw's approach dictates that "activists should not just react to crises, but use them to organize strategically."[62] As a reflective practitioner, Shaw illustrates in a series of case studies how this approach guides individuals in their organized efforts to promote social justice—whether through strategically planning, assessing politicians' actions (and promised for actions), collaborating with adjacent organizations, initiating legal action, or agitating authorities.[63] With the help of Shaw and Dewey, Eldridge explains how political technology operates on the street level: "Many advocates for social justice start with a rationally generated ideal and demand that an existing situation be replaced by one that conforms to their ideal.[64] Dewey, who was not without his ideals, would seem to side with political operatives, the political 'pragmatists,' in requiring that any suggested change take the existing situation into account and work from there. One moves the current practice toward an ideal, modifying both situation and ideal as needed, through a process of deliberative change." In other words, political technologies and democratic ideals must be adapted to the conditions of the situation and the objectives of the present inquiry, a truism that political operatives live by and Dewey respected as a constraint on his own political philosophy.

Eldridge's elaboration of Dewey's answer to Randall in terms of Shaw's recommendations for social justice activists is helpful insofar as it operationalizes what Dewey might have meant by adequate political technology. Moreover, it does so from an anthropological perspective. Eldridge treats Deweyan political technology as a form of cultural practice and habitual activity, both in "the way action is organized" and "the publicly available symbolic forms through which people experience and express meaning."[65] I strongly believe that Eldridge's scholarly work, his legacy, is worthy of close attention and inquiry by pragmatists and Dewey scholars today. His own writings on Dewey's historical engagements, pragmatic political activism, Obama's pragmatism and the many meanings of pragmatism, to name only a few topics, demonstrate rigor, honesty, and acumen that are rare.[66] Eldridge was also a scholar-teacher who continually challenged others, pressing them to ask uncomfortable questions about Dewey's life and work—not just to idolize the historical figure, but to criticize, improve, and extend his ideas in meaningful ways.[67]

Acknowledgment

I would like to acknowledge the late Michael Eldridge, a scholar and a gentleman who influenced many young Dewey scholars during his lifetime.

Notes

1. Dewey, EW, 5:93. Citations of Dewey's writings are to *The Collected Works of John Dewey: 1882–1953, electronic edition*, Past Masters, ed. Jo Ann Boydston and Larry A. Hickman (Charlottesville: Intelex Corporation, 1996). To cite specific sections, I follow the conventional method, LW (Later Works) or MW (Middle Works) or EW (Early Works), volume: page number. For example, EW 5:93 refers to the Early Works, volume 5, page 93. I also cite the original date of publication.

2. John Herman Randall, Jr. "Dewey's Interpretations of the History of Philosophy," in *The Philosophy of John Dewey*, ed. A. Schilpp (New York: Tudor Publishing Company, 1951), 82.

3. Michael Eldridge, *Transforming Experience: John Dewey's Cultural Instrumentalism* (Nashville: Vanderbilt University Press, 1998), 83.

4. Dewey, LW, 13:367.

5. Ibid.

6. Ibid.

7. Dewey, LW, 13:226.

8. Dewey, LW, 2:325.

9. Dewey, LW, 2:326.

10. I make a more detailed argument that Dewey is not a deliberative democrat, at least not in the modern sense, in "Dewey and Goodin on the Value of Monological Deliberation" and "Dewey's Theory of Moral (and Political) Deliberation Unfiltered."

11. Dewey, LW, 2:371.

12. Dewey, LW, 2:325.

13. Dewey, LW, 13:187.

14. Eldridge, *Transforming Experience,* 113.

15. Dewey, MW, 9:338.

16. Randall, "Dewey's Interpretations of the History of Philosophy," 77–102. Cited by Michael Eldridge. See note 2.

17. Dewy, LW, 14:75. Cited by Michael Eldridge. See note 2.

18. Dewey claims that in the institutional phase "[w]e acted as if democracy were something that took place mainly at Washington and Albany—or some other state capital—under the impetus of what happened when men and women went to the polls once a year or so—which is a somewhat extreme way of saying that we have had the habit of thinking of democracy as a kind of political mechanism that will work as long as citizens were reasonably faithful in performing political

duties." "Creative Democracy—The Task Before Us" (Dewy, LW, 14:225). In the ideational phase, "[t]he idea of democracy is a wider and fuller idea than can be exemplified in the state even at its best. To be realized it must affect all modes of human association, the family, the school, industry, religion" (Dewey, LW 2:325).

19. See, for instance, Robert B. Westbrook, *Democratic Hope: Pragmatism and the Politics of Truth* (Ithaca: Cornell University Press, 2005) 185; and Sheldon S. Wolin, *Politics and Vision: Continuity and Innovation in Western Political Thought* (Princeton: Princeton University Press, 2004) 512.

20. Roger T. Ames, "Tang Junyi and the Very 'Idea' of Confucian Democracy," in Democracy as Culture: Deweyan Pragmatism in a Globalizing World, ed. S. Tan and J. Whalen-Bridge (Albany: State University of New York Press, 2008), 179.

21. Frank Lentricchia describes the need for cultural criticism: "Ruling culture does not define the whole of culture, though it tries to, and it is the task of the oppositional critic to re-read culture so as to amplify and strategically position the marginalized voices of the ruled, exploited, oppressed and excluded." Lentricchia, Frank, *Criticism and Social Change*, reprint edition (Chicago: University of Chicago Press, 1985), 15.

22. This treatment of Dewey as an institutionalist closely follows my account in "Can Pragmatists be Institutionalists?"

23. By habit Dewey does not just mean a rutted channel or encrusted pattern of past behavior. Habits are live with values, virtues and possibilities for intelligent action. Dewey explains why he chose to employ the word 'habit' as the repository of both values and virtues: "But we need a word ['habit'] to express that kind of human activity which is influenced by prior activity and in that sense acquired; which contains within itself a certain ordering or systematization of minor elements of action; which is projective, dynamic in quality, ready for overt manifestation; and which is operative in some subdued subordinate form even when not obviously dominating activity" (Dewey, MW, 14:31).

24. Dewey, LW 3:153.

25. In Dewey's words, "[i]deals . . . that are not embodied in institutions are of little avail." John Dewey, "Liberating the Social Scientist," *Commentary* 4, (October 1947): 10.

26. Dewey, LW, 14:119.

27. Hegel, G W. F. (1807) 1979. The Phenomenology of Spirit. trans. A. V. Miller (Oxford: Oxford University Press.

28. Dewey credits the "Hegelian deposit" in his philosophy in his autobiographical essay "From Absolutism to Experimentalism" (Dewey, LW, 5:147–59).

29. Dewey, LW, 14:92.

30. Similar to Fukuyama, though, Dewey defines political democracy in liberal-democratic terms, that is, as those "traditional political institutions" which include "general suffrage, elected representatives, [and] majority rule" (Dewey, LW,

2:325). Frances Fukuyama, "The End of History?" *The National Interest* 16, (Summer 1989): 210, https://www.jstor.org/stable/24027184.

31. Dewey's reluctance to specify model institutions that realize his democratic ideal is mirrored in the aversion that contemporary critical theorists have to institutional design. According to Schutz, "Dewey resisted calls for him to develop a specific model of democratic government, arguing that it must look differently in different contexts." Aaron Schutz, "John Dewey and 'a Paradox of Size': Democratic Faith and the Limits of Experience," *American Journal of Education* 109, no. 3 (May 2001): 288, https://doi.org/10.1086/444273. Dryzek explains: "Overly precise specification of model institutions involves skating on thin ice. Far better, perhaps, to leave any such specification to the individual involved. The appropriate configuration will depend on the constraints and opportunities of the existing social situation, the cultural tradition(s) to which the participants subscribe, and the capabilities and desires of these actors." John Dryzek, "Discursive Designs: Critical Theory and Political Institutions," *American Journal of Political Science* 31, no. 3 (August 1987): 665, https://www.jstor.org/stable/2111287.

32. Further on, Dewey writes, "[T]he ultimate value of every institution is its distinctively human effect—its effect upon conscious experience . . ." (Dewey, MW, 9:9–10).

33. David Waddington (2008, 62)

34. James Campbell, *Understanding John Dewey: Nature and Cooperative Intelligence, International Studies in Philosophy (Chicago: Open Court Publishing Company, 1995), 201–8.*

35. Dewey, MW, 10:339 (emphasis in the original).

36. Dewey, LW, 14:96.

37. Mitchell Aboulafia, "Obama's Pragmatism and the Stimulus Package," *Up@Night* (blog), February 2, 2009, https://upnight.com/2009/02/09/obamas-pragmatism-and-the-stimulus-package/. Michael Eldridge, "Adjectival and Generic Pragmatism: Problems and Possibilities" Human Affairs 19, no. 1 (2009): 10–18, https://doi.org/10.2478/v10023-009-0015-y. Peter Levine, *The New Progressive Era: Toward a Fair and Deliberative Democracy* (Lanham: Rowman and Littlefield, 2000); and Sunstein 2008).

38. Piki Ish-Shalom, "Theorizing Politics, Politicizing Theory, and the Responsibility that Runs Between." *Perspectives on Politics* 7, no. 2 (2009): 303–16. https://www.jstor.org/stable/40406932.

39. Dewey, MW, 10:42.

40. Randall, "Dewey's Interpretations," 82.

41. Dewey, LW, 1:362–63.

42. Franz Boas, (1911) 1938, *The Mind of Primitive Man*, 2nd ed. (New York: The MacMillan Company).

43. Ibid., 196.

44. Franz Boas, "The Methods of Ethnology," *American Anthropologist* 22, no. 4 (1920): 320, https://doi.org/10.1525/aa.1920.22.4.02a00020.

45. Dewey, LW, 6:224–30.

46. Boas, *The Mind of Primitive Man*, 162–3.

47. Ibid., 163.

48. Dewey, MW, 9:338.

49. The central ideas of Dewey's lost 1884 dissertation are thought to be preserved in his essay "Kant and Philosophic Method" (Dewey, EW, 1:30–40), which was published in the same year.

50. Immanuel Kant, *Anthropology from a Pragmatic Point of View*, Cambridge Texts in the History of Philosophy, ed. Robert B. Louden (Cambridge: Cambridge University Press, 2006). Based on lectures given in 1772/73 and 1795/96.

51. Kant, *Anthropology, 7, 325.*

52. However, I would not take the next step and call Kant a "pragmatist." For a recent commentator who does, though for more methodological than substantive reasons, see Robert B. Brandom, *Perspectives on Pragmatism: Classical, Recent, and Contemporary* (Cambridge: Harvard University Press, 2011), 3–4.

53. Dewey, LW, 13:72.

54. John Dewy, *German Philosophy and Politics (Freeport: Henry Holt and Company, 1915)* https://www.questia.com/read/5749767/german-philosophy-and-politics. For commentary and analysis, see Campbell (2004) and James Scott Johnston, "Dewey's Critique of Kant." *Transactions of the Charles S. Peirce Society* 42, no. 4 (Fall 2006): 537–45, https://www.jstor.org/stable/40321348.

55. Dewey, LW, 13:367.

56. Dewey, LW, 12:21.

57. Dewey, LW, 14:15.

58. Tom Burke, *Dewey's New logic: A Reply to Russell* (Chicago: University of Chicago Press, 1994). 23.

59. Dewey, LW, 14:19–20.

60. I thank the referee for this important point.

61. Though more empirically oriented than Shaw's handbook, John Bowers and Donovan Ochs' study of political activism in the 1960s also has a Deweyan spirit to it. They examined the rhetorical strategies employed by social movement participants in advocating for social change, from petitioning authorities to promulgating their ideas in public forums, solidifying their base of support with slogans and symbols of solidarity, to non-violent resistance, and finally to escalating and confronting authorities in ways that prompt members of the establishment to overreact and humiliate themselves. See John W. Bowers and Donavan J. Ochs. *The Rhetoric of Agitation and Control* (Boston: Addison Wesley Publishers, 1971), 16–28.

62. Eldridge, *Transforming Experience*, 118.

63. Ibid., 118–19.

64. Ibid., 120.

65. Ann Swidler, "Culture in Action: Symbols and Strategies," *American Sociological Review* 51, no. 2 (1986): 273–76, https://doi.org//10.2307/2095521

66. Eldridge, *Transforming Experience;* Eldridge, "Adjectival and Generic Pragmatism"; and Michael Eldridge "Linking Obama's Pragmatism to Philosophical Pragmatism: Obama as a Pragmatic Democrat." *Contemporary Pragmatism* 8, no. 2 (2011): 113–21, https://doi.org/10.1163/18758185-90000205.

67. This is a task that I humbly tried to accomplish in my first book, dedicated to Eldridge, titled *John Dewey's Great Debates—Reconstructed.*

Bibliography

Aboulafia, Mitchell. "Obama's Pragmatism and the Stimulus Package." *Up@ Night* (blog), February 2, 2009. https://upnight.com/2009/02/09/obamas -pragmatism-and-the-stimulus-package/.

Ames, Roger T. "Tang Junyi and the Very 'Idea' of Confucian Democracy." In *Democracy as Culture: Deweyan Pragmatism in a Globalizing World*, edited by S. Tan and J. Whalen-Bridge, 177–200. Albany: State University of New York Press, 2008.

Apple, Michael W. *Ideology and Curriculum*. Boston: Routledge & Kegan Paul, 1979.

Boas, Franz. "The Methods of Ethnology." *American Anthropologist* 22, no. 4 (1920): 311–21. https://*doi*.org/10.1525/aa.1920.22.4.02a00020.

———. (1911) 1938. *The Mind of Primitive Man*, 2nd ed. New York: The MacMillan Company.

Bowers, John W. and Donavan J. Ochs. *The Rhetoric of Agitation and Control*. Boston: Addison Wesley Publishers, 1971.

Brandom, Robert B. *Perspectives on Pragmatism: Classical, Recent, and Contemporary*. Cambridge: Harvard University Press, 2011.

Burke, Tom. *Dewey's New Logic: A Reply to Russell*. Chicago: University of Chicago Press, 1994.

Campbell, James. *Understanding John Dewey: Nature and Cooperative Intelligence, International Studies in Philosophy*. Chicago: Open Court Publishing Company, 1995.

———. Dewey, John. *German Philosophy and Politics*. Freeport: Henry Holt and Company, 1915. https://www.questia.com/read/5749767/german-philosophy -and-politics.

———. "Dewey and German Philosophy in Wartime." *Transactions of the Charles S. Peirce Society* 40, no. 1 (Winter 2004): 1–20. https://www.jstor.org /stable/40320972.

Dewey, John. "Liberating the Social Scientist." *Commentary* 4, (October 1947): 379–85.

———. *The Collected Works of John Dewey: 1882–1953, electronic edition*, Past Masters, edited by Jo Ann Boydston and Larry A. Hickman. Charlottesville: Intelex Corporation, 1996.

Dryzek, John S. "Discursive Designs: Critical Theory and Political Institutions." *American Journal of Political Science* 31, no. 3 (August 1987): 656–79. https://www.jstor.org/stable/2111287.

Eldridge, Michael. *Transforming Experience: John Dewey's Cultural Instrumentalism*. Nashville: Vanderbilt University Press, 1998.

———. "Adjectival and Generic Pragmatism: Problems and Possibilities." *Human Affairs* 19, no. 1 (2009): 10–8. https://doi.org/10.2478/v10023-009-0015-y.

———. "Linking Obama's Pragmatism to Philosophical Pragmatism: Obama as a Pragmatic Democrat." *Contemporary Pragmatism* 8, no. 2 (2011): 113–21. https://doi.org/10.1163/18758185-90000205.

Fukuyama, Frances. "The End of History?" *The National Interest* 16, (Summer 1989): 3–18. https://www.jstor.org/stable/24027184.

Hegel, G. W. F. (1807) 1979. *The Phenomenology of Spirit*. Translated by A. V. Miller. Oxford: Oxford University Press.

Ish-Shalom, Piki. "Theorizing Politics, Politicizing Theory, and the Responsibility that Runs Between." *Perspectives on Politics*, 7, no. 2 (2009): 303–16. https://www.jstor.org/stable/40406932.

Jackson, Philip Wesley. *Life in Classrooms*. New York: Holt, Rinehart, and Winston, 1968.

Johnston, James Scott. "Dewey's Critique of Kant." *Transactions of the Charles S. Peirce Society* 42, no. 4 (Fall 2006): 518–51. https://www.jstor.org/stable/40321348.

Kant, Immanuel. *Anthropology from a Pragmatic Point of View*, Cambridge Texts in the History of Philosophy. Edited by Robert B. Louden. Cambridge: Cambridge University Press, 2006.

Lentricchia, Frank. *Criticism and Social Change*, reprint edition. Chicago: University of Chicago Press, 1985.

Levine, Peter. *The New Progressive Era: Toward a Fair and Deliberative Democracy*. Lanham: Rowman and Littlefield, 2000.

Ralston, Shane. J. "Can Pragmatists be Institutionalists? John Dewey Joins the Non-Ideal/Ideal Theory Debate." *Human Studies* 33, no. 1 (May 2010): 65–84. https://www.jstor.org/stable/40981090.

———. "Dewey and Goodin on the Value of Monological Deliberation." *Etica & Politica* 12, no. 1 (2010): 235–55. http://www2.units.it/etica/2010_1/EP_2010_1.pdf#page=235.

———. "Dewey's Theory of Moral (and Political) Deliberation Unfiltered." *Education and Culture* 26, no. 1 (2010): 23–43. https://doi.org/10.1353/eac.0.0049.

———. *John Dewey's Great Debates—Reconstructed*. Charlotte: Information Age Publishing, 2011.

Randall, John Herman, Jr. "Dewey's Interpretations of the History of Philosophy." In *The Philosophy of John Dewey*, edited by A. Schilpp, 77–102. New York: Tudor Publishing Company, 1951.

Schultz, B. "Obama's Political Philosophy: Pragmatism, Politics, and the University of Chicago." *Philosophy of the Social Sciences* 39, no. 2 (2009): 127–73. https://doi.org/10.1177/0048393109332453.

Schutz, Aaron. "John Dewey and 'a Paradox of Size': Democratic Faith and the Limits of Experience." *American Journal of Education* 109, no. 3 (May 2001): 287–319. https://doi.org/10.1086/444273.

Shaw, Randy. *The Activist's Handbook: A Primer for the 1990's and Beyond*, second edition. Berkeley: University of California Press, 1996.

Sunstein, Cass R. "The Empiricist Strikes Back: Obama's Pragmatism Explained." *The New Republic*, 10 (September 2008).

Swidler, Ann. "Culture in Action: Symbols and Strategies." *American Sociological Review* 51, no. 2 (1986): 273–86. https://doi.org/10.2307/2095521.

Waddington, David I. "John Dewey: Closet Conservative." *Paideusis*, 17, no. 2 (2008): 51-63.

Westbrook, Robert B. *Democratic Hope: Pragmatism and the Politics of Truth*. Ithaca: Cornell University Press, 2005.

Wolin, Sheldon S. *Politics and Vision: Continuity and Innovation in Western Political Thought*. Princeton: Princeton University Press, 2004.

Shane J. Ralston is an affiliate advisor at Woolf University.

BORDENTOWN: WHERE DEWEY'S "LEARNING TO EARN" MET DU BOISIAN EDUCATIONAL PRIORITIES

*The Unique Legacy of a Once Thriving but
Largely Forgotten School for Black Students*

Connie Goddard

ABSTRACT

John Dewey and W.E.B. Du Bois were prominent critics of how vocational education programs were often used to restrict rather than enhance student aspirations. An overview of the Bordentown Manual Training and Industrial School for Colored Youth (1886–1955) suggests that it met requirements both men articulated for the right kind of vocational education; however, the school's legacy has been largely ignored by historians. Further, Dewey and Du Bois, who knew of but had little interaction with each other, may never have discussed their shared interest in vocational education or their awareness of the school's mission and accomplishments.

On February 20 of 1917, John Dewey addressed a meeting of the Public Education Association in New York City with a paper about vocational education, a topic of particular interest at the time—the Smith–Hughes Act would be signed by President Woodrow Wilson a few days later. The following month, his paper would be published as "Learning to Earn: The Place of Vocational Education in a Comprehensive Scheme of Public Education" in *School & Society*.[1] Of concern to Dewey and many other progressives at the time was whether the potential virtues of this early piece of federal aid to schools would chiefly serve the interests of students or those of employers: would the funds support vocational education in comprehensive secondary schools, which Dewey advocated, or would it foster a dual system of schools, which business leaders tended to prefer?

W.E.B. Du Bois, a decade younger than Dewey, had begun writing about vocational education a decade or more before Dewey—most famously in his chapter on Booker T. Washington in *The Souls of Black Folk*, published in 1903.[2] Though the Du Bois Archives include several letters mentioning vocational education written during the decade before Dewey's talk, there are none that refer to the Smith-Hughes Act or to Dewey's strong feelings on the topic.[3] The two did meet on a few occasions, most prominently at the National Negro Conference in May 1909. According to David Levering Lewis's account of that gathering, neither spoke specifically about vocational education, though their talks did touch on related subjects. Dewey claimed that racism denied the nation of "social capital"; Du Bois lectured the gathering—1500 or so black and white academics and reformers—on the connection between racism and cheap labor.[4]

At the time of Dewey's speech, he was likely at least vaguely aware of a school about 65 miles south of where he was speaking, a school that would embody his ideas about a comprehensive high school. As his talk was a classic, the school— the Manual Training and Industrial School for Colored Youth (MTIS)—ought to be widely hailed as a classic, too, as an icon of progressive ideas, particularly for the manner in which it would merge academic courses with vocational training. Urged to visit the school by the Philadelphia art collector Albert Barnes (who was a friend of Du Bois as well), he apparently did in March of 1928, but no record of his reaction has yet been found.[5] In 1922, Du Bois gave a talk at the school titled "The Choice of a Vocation," in which he discussed the considerations that should go into choosing one's life work.[6] Though we can only speculate as to what these considerations were, Du Bois visited the school several times over the next decade or more and was apparently impressed by what he saw, thus we might assume that the school met Du Boisian criteria.[7] These, Derrick Alridge set out both in a 1999 article and in his 2008 book on Du Bois's thoughts about education. In the latter, Alridge wrote that "Dewey and Du Bois were, in many ways, of like mind and spirit" and "held similar views on many educational issues," but whether they ever discussed how well the Bordentown school fulfilled their expectations may never be known.[8]

Despite this celebrity attention a century ago, the school is largely unknown today. Though MTIS had closed in 1955, in the wake of *Brown v. Board of Education*, its once-elegant campus still exists, albeit in considerable disrepair; in the decades since then, it has been used as both a mental health and a correctional facility. Often called simply "Bordentown" for the New Jersey town where it had been established— on a bluff high above the Delaware River—the school would eventually abound with ideas that enhanced the self-confidence of its students and their ability to contribute to their communities. Dewey may have known of MTIS because its new principal, William R. Valentine, had earlier attracted his attention—he had headed a school in Indianapolis lauded by a chapter in *Schools of Tomorrow*. Titled "The School as a Social Settlement," the chapter praised the close relationship between the school's program and the poor, black, under-resourced community it served—students ran a soup kitchen, repaired their families' shoes in the cobbler's shop, rebuilt and maintained the school's buildings, and even ran a small bank. The school had become an integral part of its community and residents valued it as such.[9]

As a sign, no doubt, of the Bordentown school's anonymity, it is not mentioned in a 2009 article about P.S. 26, as the Indianapolis school was known, an article that takes Dewey to task for having too narrow a European-American view of students, classrooms, and communities. This argument, though well-reasoned and scholarly, might be labelled as demonstrating a bit of "presentism"—judging an institution that thrived a century ago by a set of standards that have emerged out of contemporary concerns and insights.[10] MTIS, often labelled "Tuskegee of the North," offered a less regimented and more forward-looking education than that provided in Booker T. Washington's institution.[11] But, like P.S. 26, MTIS started where the students were—its faculty, educated at some of the nation's best colleges, guided their students in the direction they thought led to success in society at that time.[12]

A decade ago, Bordentown attracted the attention of a documentary film company, which produced an admiring portrait of the school called *A Place Out of Time*. The video combined historical footage along with filmed memories by the school's fond graduates, who gathered frequently to celebrate their years there.[13] In October of 2002, many had come to celebrate the school's being placed on the National Register of Historic Places.[14] The school was the subject of two doctoral dissertations, one of which was written by a Bordentown graduate.[15] Another dissertation, offering oral histories of segregated schooling in New Jersey, includes memories of MTIS.[16] Of note, none of these mention either Dewey or Du Bois. However, Marion Thompson Wright, in her standard-setting book on education for blacks in New Jersey, comments on the school's effectiveness in ways that suggest her familiarity with social reconstructionists during her doctoral work at Teachers College in the 1930s.[17]

An informal check of several standard histories of education and encyclopedias of African American history turned up no mention of the school or of William Valentine; also surprising is that an index to the *Journal of Negro Education,* to which both Wright and Du Bois contributed, includes no reference to either MTIS or its principal.[18] The school has been receiving some recent attention, though. A granddaughter of the school's founder recently published a book on the school's lessons for today.[19] Two other scholars are currently studying the school and William Valentine, asserting that both deserve recognition as progressive icons.[20]

A brief history of MTIS suggests ways in which the school honored priorities articulated by both Dewey and Du Bois, particularly during the first two decades of Valentine's leadership. Juxtaposing ideas of those two great educators through a story of the school headed by the third, Valentine, suggests that the Bordentown legacy deserves more attention.

SETTING THE SCHOOL IN TIME, PLACE, AND IDEOLOGY

Though often compared with Tuskegee, MTIS never became a post-secondary school. However, like Tuskegee, it ought to be seen through a broad historical lens. Both schools were established during the 1880s, when there was considerable interest nationwide in manual training programs for public high schools. Lawrence Cremin, in his history of progressivism, wrote that differences in how to approach such programs "became the crux of the most vigorous pedagogical battle of the 1880s." On one side were traditionalists who believed that public schools should focus on a "cultural education useful to all"; others felt that some knowledge of trades and handicrafts should "be part of a balanced general education."[21] So, yes, Tuskegee had been established in 1881 as an outcome of Washington's experience at the Hampton Institute, but the relevance of manual training for all students, black and white, was broadly supported by educators nationwide. The issue, as Dewey frequently asserted during the decade in which Valentine arrived, was the kind of manual training and its goal. His "An Undemocratic Proposal" of 1913 argued that a proposal under consideration in Illinois, which would have established a separate high school system for vocational students, would have resulted in programs that benefited industries rather than students. In a 1914 article, Dewey expressed his dismay that a national commission on vocational education included legislators and business owners—but no educators.[22]

In the spring of 1915—shortly before Valentine arrived as MTIS principal— Dewey had engaged in a spirited debate with vocational education advocate David Snedden; Dewey argued that the latter's proposals would "put a fence around industrial education," separating vocational students from those in general education programs; thus the plan would not serve democratic purposes. Snedden's response was that such a fence used the nation's resources more efficiently; thus his program would be more democratic.[23]

Du Bois also wrote about the strengths and shortcomings of vocational education during this period, perhaps most notably in his critical review of Thomas Jesse Jones's massive study of education for Negroes, published in 1916. Of interest here is that neither Jones's study nor Du Bois's review mention Dewey.[24] Similarly, during this decade, in his numerous writings about vocational education, Dewey did not specifically address the unique circumstance that applied to black students, though some of his comments about the injustice of separating vocational education for academic students could be read as opposition to segregation in general.[25] In his compelling study of Dewey's evolving understanding of race, Thomas Fallace suggests that Dewey's "linear historicism" of the 1890s had matured into a cultural pluralism by 1920.[26] As the two men moved in similar circles—both play a significant role in Louis Menand's *The Metaphysical Club*—it's difficult to view the limited communication between Dewey and Du Bois as less than a great misfortune.[27] And it raises the question as to whether manual training might have taken off on a different trajectory, for black students as well as white, had there been communication on the topic between the two.

The Bordentown school had been founded in 1886 by a visionary minister, the Rev. Walter Allen Rice; with modest financial backing from a Technical and Industrial Education Association, Rev. Rice and his wife opened a small boarding school in a few wooden buildings 10 miles south of Trenton. Their concern was for children, girls as well as boys, from unstable homes—"colored" children at the time were not welcome in Bordentown's other public schools. Their goal was to equip them to earn a living, a particular challenge in those decades of restricted opportunities for African Americans. In the mid-1890s, the state of New Jersey took over the school, which had been struggling on private donations.[28] Referred to as a "star of hope" by the state superintendent of instruction, the school and its forty or so students were moved to an estate one mile south of Bordentown.[29] It officially became the Manual Training and Industrial School for Colored Youth; James Gregory—formerly a professor at Howard University—was named the new principal, buildings were constructed, and programs established.[30]

Under Gregory's leadership, the school hovered between following the manual training model advocated by Washington and becoming a more academic institution. While the state may have envisioned the former—by 1900, carpentry, farming, dressmaking, and laundry were among the trades taught—Gregory, a noted classics scholar and activist who shared many acquaintances with Du Bois, wanted to aim for a more academic program.[31] When illness forced him to resign in 1915, he is reported to have said that he didn't feel equipped to lead a trade school.[32]

In 1913, New Jersey's new commissioner of education, Calvin Kendall, had invited Booker T. Washington to visit the school and make recommendations.[33] Washington suggested that the school should focus on the "prevailing occupations" in the black community, which at the time were largely in agriculture and domestic service.[34] Academic work, however, ought "not to be neglected," he wrote; instead it should be "dovetailed into these practical industries [that give] a more severe mental training than . . . abstract old-form book education."[35] Though there are surface similarities with the work of "occupations" that Dewey had articulated in *The School and Society*, Washington's concept of "dovetailing" was more rigid than what Dewey had proposed a dozen years earlier.[36]

For Kendall, Gregory's resignation provided an opportunity for him to bring to Bordentown a young man he had known while superintendent of schools in Indianapolis, William Valentine.[37] It was an inspired appointment. Though born in Virginia, Valentine had graduated from high school in Montclair, New Jersey, and from Harvard in 1904. Tall, slim, and elegant in appearance, Valentine could easily handle the tension inherent to the job. As the late Rutgers historian Clement Price has noted, "Black leaders between World Wars I and II were craftsmen in negotiating the best interests of the race without appearing to be Uncle Toms, but at the same time recognizing, respecting the racial hierarchy."[38]

Of his career, Valentine reported to his Harvard classmates in their 25th reunion album: "Contrary to expectation, I landed in the education field in Indianapolis immediately following my graduation. . . . In those early days, I acquired a conviction that the public school was a social agent to serve its community somewhat in the manner of a settlement house, and in fact to take its place." He wrote that he "experimented with that notion with some success" in Indianapolis, and then notes that his work there had gained the attention of "Dr. John Dewey."[39] Valentine remained MTIS principal until 1950, becoming in the process one of the most well-known African Americans in the state.[40] In 1928, he earned a master's degree at Teachers College, Columbia; a decade later, he was awarded an honorary doctorate from Lincoln University in Pennsylvania.[41]

VALENTINE'S PLANS FOR BORDENTOWN

The ideas Valentine had begun to develop in Indianapolis he brought with him when he went to Bordentown—and during the three and a half decades of his leadership, MTIS grew from a modest middle school with 90 or so students into a thriving secondary school that enrolled over 400 students and served as a cultural center for New Jersey's black community.[42] Eventually the campus included 400 acres, two dozen Georgian brick buildings, a working farm, orchards, tennis courts, athletic fields, and a parade ground. If, prior to his arrival, the school had struggled to decide whether it would be an academic institution or focus on more practical skills, under Valentine, it became both.[43] In 1926, MTIS published a booklet titled "A Decade of Progress"—printed by the student-staffed print shop—which offered details on the school's growth. The booklet noted that applications had "poured in," and at the time there were 320 students, 189 of whom were boys.[44] In 1926, the state gave the school permission to offer a full high school program.

By 1930, that secondary program was well underway.[45] Students could opt for either an academic and trade program or a trade program alone, and they had considerable choice over which program and what trades they would take up. The school week was divided into 10 segments; for five half-days, students focused on academic subjects. Both those headed for further education and those aiming for a diploma and trade certificate alone took a standard high school program of English, history and civics, and math and science. For four of the other half-days, students learned a trade through which they could earn a living—for girls, these were mainly being a seamstress or a beautician; for boys, mainly auto mechanics and building maintenance. In the remaining half-day per week, students helped to maintain the school—doing carpentry, laundry, or meal service; tending to the school's prize-winning cattle or working in its gardens and orchards.[46] The school had, in Dewey's terms, a program that was "unit" rather than "dual."

On the weekends, students were offered a rich array of cultural activities, and many got to tour with the school's athletic teams, bands, and choirs.[47] One of the school's major functions was its annual Memorial Day festivities, which featured its military-style cadet corps, its prize-winning choirs and bands, and speeches by honored guests (who included at various times Mary McLeod Bethune, Paul Robeson, Albert Einstein, and Eleanor Roosevelt).[48] Though families paid for school uniforms and contributed to room and board, MTIS was otherwise funded by the state. In 1940, students were expected to pay approximately $175 per year to attend.[49]

Thus, Valentine led the development of a self-contained community, amply supported by a well-qualified faculty and staff—also all black—who lived on campus; many of them remained throughout Valentine's tenure, providing emotional support and modeling the goals and behavior they wanted to instill in students. Faculty members had degrees from a variety of distinctive schools, including Bates, Amherst, Radcliffe, Wellesley, Harvard, Rutgers, Howard, Fisk, and Tuskegee. Among them were three holders of Phi Beta Kappa keys. All were fully state-certified, including those who taught the vocational courses. They were also well paid in comparison with prevailing salaries in other schools, but living on campus, they were expected to be available to students for much of the day.[50] Bordentown graduates interviewed for *A Place Out of Time* praised the role of the faculty; one claimed that they "nurtured and cuddled" us; when appropriate, they also "kicked us in the butt."[51]

MTIS STUDENTS LEARN TO EARN—AND TO BE ENTREPRENEURIAL

Though Frank Margonis and Thomas Fallace have both reviewed P.S. 26 in Indianapolis through a Deweyan lens, this may be the first effort to similarly review MTIS.[52] One means to do so is by evaluating it through the criteria provided by Dewey's 1917 "Learning to Earn" article.[53] Though Dewey made infrequent mention of the challenges blacks faced at the time, the goals and principles Valentine sought to instill at MTIS resonate in the former's arguments.[54] If Dewey's goal was to make students masters of their fate, MTIS aimed to do the same. "Learning to Earn" begins with the assertion that "popular education has always been rather largely vocational"; schools existed to prepare students for the work they would do as adults.[55] The fundamental question was whether such schooling existed primarily to serve the long-term needs of the employers or of the employed. MTIS, despite the constraints under which it operated, put its focus on the latter.[56]

The body of Dewey's article discussed five distinctions, which he posed as negatives; the differences between these and their more beneficial opposites he described as the "great difference between the happiness which means merely contentment with a station and the happiness which comes from the struggle of a well-equipped person to better his station." Thus, how well did MTIS accomplish Dewey's goals?

- *Did it offer "an education which will enable employees to fit better into the existing economic scheme" or did it provide an education more beneficial for students' long-term needs?*

Dewey raised this consideration in light of current discussion about the Smith-Hughes Act—would it result in the dual set of schools that Dewey opposed? Though MTIS did exist within a dual system, it was one based more on race rather than on class: school segregation was officially prohibited in New Jersey, but the practice became more widespread with the growth of the black population during the Great Migration.[57] Thus, Bordentown had to deal with two dual systems—one in schools and the other in the workplace. Blacks were denied union jobs, could get only maintenance roles in factories, and if they acquired a definite skill, they were often limited to selling it within black communities.[58]

As the black population grew, there were more opportunities for MTIS graduates to provide specialized services—auto and building maintenance, dressmaking, and eventually cosmetology and auto mechanics.[59] Even during the Great Depression, graduates reported having little difficulty finding work in fields they were prepared to enter.[60] The MTIS curriculum, thus, dealt progressively with the economic conditions of the times—and endeavored to prepare students to work within the system but not "to fall docilely into the subordinate ranks of the industrial army," as Dewey worried that students in a corporate-sponsored program would do.

- *Was the program's "primary object . . . merely to prepare more skilled workers for the present system" or to prepare them to change the system?*

Despite Washington's 1913 advice, Bordentown students had limited interest in agricultural jobs. In a 1927 publication, MTIS celebrated the work of its graduates; of 309 who completed a survey conducted in 1925, only six men reported being farmers or gardeners. Instead, they were auto mechanics and drivers, machinists and musicians, carpenters and teachers. Women were primarily dressmakers, housewives, nurses, social workers, and teachers. Many of both sexes were still in school, which could have meant finishing high school as well as going on for more education. Furthermore, a substantial number owned their owned businesses—a garage, a cartage service, an electrical supply store, a building design and construction firm.[61]

This independent, entrepreneurial tendency of MTIS graduates continued for the rest of the school's existence.[62] Yearbooks for the classes of 1953 to 1955 note the career aspirations of its graduates. Many of the women wanted to be nurses, social workers, or teachers; others aimed to be beauticians or dressmakers, dancers or singers; a few aspired to be physicians and one wanted to be a lawyer. Among the men, career aspirations were equally varied: mechanics and engineers predominated; several aimed to be architects and designers. A few wanted to be athletes or musicians; several others expressed interest in fields in which they might be self-employed: a mortician and a barber among them.[63] Thus, given constraints of the time, students' aspirations suggest that they wanted to define, within limits, their own role in the world.

- *Did the school's curriculum "neglect as useless . . . the topics in history and civics which make future workers aware of their rightful claims as citizens of a democracy"—or does it instill in them democratic instincts?*

On this distinction, the MTIS program would surely have met with Dewey's approval. From 1927 on, the academic program consisted of what was standard for high schools across the country; further, students who did not intend to go on for more education were required to take one year of "Negro history."[64] Both in the formal courses they took, and through the informal but steady mentoring they received from the faculty, students absorbed pride and self-discipline; they knew the limitations a racist society imposed on them, but they also knew their rights and responsibilities as citizens.[65]

Further, through the organizations and cultural enrichment they participated in, students acquired other qualities Dewey valued, such as studies that "fit the individual for the reasonable enjoyment of leisure," and that develop an "appreciation of the arts." Dewey was particularly adamant that schooling should offer all students the same exposure to literature and the arts that wealthy families were able to give their children. A member of the class of 1953, who became a college administrator after working as a beautician, claimed "everything we needed was there" when discussing the opportunities Bordentown provided.[66]

- *Did "the method and spirit" of the school "emphasize all that is most routine and automatic in our present system"—or its opposite?*

In making this distinction, Dewey had in mind assembly-line work and the various kinds of manual labor most working people did at the time. To an extent, the distinction made little difference to most Bordentown students, particularly in its early years, because black people had limited access to such jobs in industry. Dewey's "[d]rill to secure skill in the performance of tasks under the direction of others" was not a major issue for Bordentown graduates. But taking pride in one's own skills—abilities honed though the supervision of a talented and dedicated faculty while they were MTIS students—was.[67]

- *Did the school "measure its achievements" by the number of graduates it places in jobs or "by the number whom it succeeds in keeping in school" until they are "equipped to seek and find their own congenial occupations?"*

As suggested above, Bordentown's graduates felt themselves prepared to "find their own congenial occupations"; it also did well in graduating students who could find and keep a job. A survey of its class of 1935, done six months after graduation, found that 68% were working full-time, 20% were continuing their education, and only 12% were either working part time or unemployed—the Depression was still on and many others, particularly African Americans, were at best marginally employed.[68] Furthermore, Marion Wright, in her history of education for blacks in the state, wrote in 1941 that the "school had made it possible to place a larger number of Negroes in the skilled and semi-skilled trades than any other occupational unit in New Jersey."[69]

Manifesting Du Boisian Priorities

In Derrick Alridge's 1999 article proposing a Du Boisian education, he notes a priority both Dewey and Du Bois shared: "The major role that Dewey and Du Bois played during their lifetimes was to challenge America to live up to its claims of democracy and to use education as a model for and means to a more democratic society."[70] The "Du Boisian model" Alridge posits contains six elements; consciously or not, MTIS addressed several.

- *An African American Centered Education:* Learning something of African and Negro culture, Du Bois believed, could help students address notions of Negro inferiority and hopelessness.[71] Though they were living in a segregated society, MTIS, with its well-educated, all-black faculty, could counteract some of the hostility that black students so often encountered in predominantly white institutions.[72] The Bordentown school celebrated aspects of the African American culture that was developing around them; many participated in singing groups that celebrated spirituals, others in a jazz band; and the campus was frequently visited by leading black musicians, athletes, and educators.[73]

- *A Communal Education*: One of the distinctions of the Bordentown school was its being a self-contained community; students worked closely with the farm and maintenance staff to care for the livestock, harvest produce, do laundry, and make repairs to buildings and vehicles. Du Bois's argument was that a Jim Crow environment offered opportunities for blacks to exercise some control over their social and economic situation and build a strong economic infrastructure.[74] Though there are obvious limitations when analogized to MTIS, nevertheless the school offered numerous opportunities for students to acquire these skills.

- *A Broad-Based Education*: In discussing his proposal, Alridge focuses on the 1930s, because, as he argues, it's "the most ignored period in the study of Du Bois's thinking."[75] It's also the decade in which MTIS flourished, and the school was attracting some of the state's most promising students.[76] At this time, Alridge says, Du Bois realized that the "agendas of classical education or vocational education alone were far too simplistic to meet the demands of the cultural, economic, and technological changes occurring" at the time.[77] With a curriculum that provided both a strong academic program and substantial practice in job-related skills, along with a great variety of cultural and extracurricular activities, MTIS offered an admirably broad education.[78]

- *Group Leadership Education*: During the 1930s, Alridge argues, Du Bois revisited his idea of the "talented tenth" and replaced it with a "new program for Negro leadership [that he called] the 'Guiding Hundreth.'" This "does not place a greater value on occupations such as law, medicine," and other such fields; instead it "places leadership responsibility on all members of the community."[79] Unlike other noted segregated schools such as Washington, DC's famed Dunbar High, MTIS did not produce leading attorneys, scientists, and public intellectuals.[80] Instead, it produced solid members of a black middle class, which, as some black writers noted, was needed at the time.[81]

Alridge's two other aspects of a Du Boisian education—Pan-Africanism and Global Education—seem more challenges for educators in our day than they would have been during the heyday of the Bordentown school. He ends his essay with a question both Du Bois and Dewey asked a century ago: what are we going to teach our children, particularly if our goal is to extend the benefits of a democratic society to a broader range of its citizens?

THE SCHOOL CLOSES, BUT LIVES ON IN MEMORIES

After 1947, when the state's new constitution banned segregation, MTIS was under pressure to attract white students. Though that was unsuccessful, the school did attract some negative attention from vocal critics who saw it as a trade school offering outdated curricula and insisting on outmoded decorum.[82] In 1948, Valentine defended the school's reputation in a *New York Times* article. In response to this criticism, he claimed that MTIS faced a crisis "not of finances, but ideals and policy." Valentine's program for the school, the reporter wrote, "is primarily devoted to teaching by deed as much as by books, and to glorifying every achievement that would bring a child a feeling of dignity and self-respect."[83]

At the same time, Valentine put his thoughts into a brief "Statement of Philosophy" for the school. If Dewey and Du Bois wanted schools that could prepare students, both black and white, to be masters of their social and economic fate, that's what Valentine felt MTIS was offering. Under the guidance of "well-trained and understanding personnel," the "physical and social environment of the school" should lead the student to know that the individual "is not divided into compartments . . . but he is an integrated whole." The subject matter is "simply one of the tools for carrying out these purposes." The hope is that the student "will acquire a taste of success in some field of endeavor, which will motivate his aspirations and widen his horizons."[84]

Two years later, in 1950, Valentine retired, and a new principal arrived whose "unpleasant task" was to "preside over the institution's closing."[85] Despite the pall that might have descended on the school during this time, students who attended then did not seem to have been negatively affected.[86] Its last year unfolded amidst considerable controversy, with a Democratic governor insisting that it be closed because it could not attract white pupils and a Republican state Assembly insisting that it could be integrated.[87] The governor won, but his comments at the press conference announcing his decision suggested that he was not very familiar with the school's mission and accomplishments: "There is nothing to justify the existence of this school. I think any educator would tell you that Bordentown is not much of an educational institution. It isn't very high grade," he claimed.[88]

Dewey had died three years earlier; his concerns had moved beyond education, and there is no way of knowing whether he ever followed the school's history. At the time of the school's closing, Du Bois's chief concern was harassment by some government officials for his political views. As a biographer of Ella Flagg Young— who taught Dewey much of what he knew about how schools functioned— I believe she would have applauded the school's intentions and accomplishments, even if she disapproved of the segregation that made it necessary.[89] She surely shared their ideas about the role of manual education in public schools of their day, and she also had far more experience than he did in managing a school system as it attempted to absorb students of diverse backgrounds.[90] In *Isolation in the School,* she tells of a "superintendent"—presumably herself —being chastised by a group of black club women for the patronizing attitude toward former slaves evident in school textbooks.[91] Other sources suggest she learned that lesson well.[92] Though it's likely that Dewey's comments about the Bordentown experience will never be known, it seems fair to assume that he would not have shared the governor's opinions about the education the school provided. Du Bois, critic that he was of narrow trade training, might have found the governor's comments patronizing. Young, whose goal it was to move all controversies to a higher plane of thought, might have wished Albert Barnes had succeeded in getting his two friends to tour the campus together.

ACKNOWLEDGMENTS

Thanks to John R. Medley, MTIS graduate and archivist, and to many others in Trenton and Chicago.

NOTES

1. John Dewey, "Learning to Earn: The Place of Vocational Education in a Comprehensive Scheme of Public Education," *School and Society* 5, no. 117 (March 24, 1917): 331–35.

2. W.E.B. Du Bois, *The Souls of Black Folk* (1903; reprint, New York: Bantam Books, 1989).

3. W.E.B. Du Bois Papers, Special Collections and University Archives, University of Massachusetts, Amherst, Libraries.

4. David Levering Lewis, *W.E.B. Du Bois: Biography of a Race, 1868–1919* (New York: Henry Holt & Company, 1993), 392–93. In 1929, both men attended a meeting of the League for Independent Political Action in New York City.

5. A recently discovered note in the school's archives cites a "Principal's report" that refers to this visit; further information about it might be available

in the school's reports to the New Jersey board of education. In a June 14, 2018, email, Larry Hickman (emeritus director of the Dewey Center, Southern Illinois University) wrote that Barnes had persuaded Dewey to visit the school, but that a chronology of his career made no note of his having done so. Of note—in 1928, Teachers College awarded the MTIS principal William R. Valentine a master's degree. Perhaps Valentine had invited Dewey there while on the Columbia campus.

6. *New York Age*, "Du Bois speaks at Bordentown," August 18, 1922.

7. In her recent article about the school, Zoë Burkholder refers to several visits Du Bois made to the campus, citing records in the Du Bois's archive at the University of Massachusetts, Amherst, Libraries. See "'Integrated Out of Existence': African American Debates over School Integration versus Separation at the Bordentown School in New Jersey, 1886–1955," *Journal of Social History* 51, no. 1 (Fall 2017): 47–79. She claims that Du Bois tried to get the *Nation* to publish an article about the school, but that it declined to do so.

8. Derrick P. Alridge, *The Educational Thought of W.E.B. Du Bois: An Intellectual History* (New York: Teachers College Press, 2008), 41–42. Alridge claims that Du Bois tried to get Dewey to write for *The Crisis*, but that the latter never responded to those requests. See also, Alridge, "Conceptualizing a Du Boisean Philosophy of Education: Toward a Model for African-American Education," *Educational Theory* 49, no. 3 (Summer 1999): 359–379.

9. John Dewey and Evelyn Dewey, *Schools of Tomorrow* (1915; reprint, with an introduction by William W. Brickman, New York: E.P. Dutton & Co., 1962). In *The One Best System,* David Tyack wrote that the black community in Indianapolis had insisted [at around the time Valentine arrived] on having black teachers in schools for their children (Cambridge: Harvard University Press, 1974), 116.

10. Frank Margonis, "John Dewey's Racialized Visions of the Students and Classroom Community," *Educational Theory* 59, no. 1 (2009): 17–39. (This was written before Thomas Fallace's book on Dewey's evolving ideas about race appeared; see note 26. This book might have altered some of Margonis's arguments.)

11. The first printed reference to this comparison that I am aware of is in Ruth Seinfel's, "N.J. Negro School Makes Its Own World," *New York Evening Post*, December 30, 1930. Copy in the New Jersey State Archives, Trenton, SED MA01, Box 1. Subsequent references to this archive will be given as NJSA.

12. This point is made by Arthur L. Symes, a 1953 graduate, in "A Reflection on Bordentown," *Diversity* (May 13, 2016), http://discovernjhistory.org/nj-blog/.

13. *A Place Out of Time: The Bordentown School*, directed by Dave Davidson (Bethel, CT: Hudson West Productions, 2009), DVD.

14. Mildred L. Rice Jordan, *Reclaiming African-American Students: Legacies, Lessons, and Prescriptions, The Bordentown School Model.* (Bloomington, IN: iUniverse, 2017), 113.

15. Ezola Bolden Adams, "The Role and Function of the Manual Training and Industrial School at Bordentown as an Alternative School, 1915–1955" (Ed.D. diss., Rutgers University, 1977); Adams attended ca. 1950; and Evelyn Blackmore Duck, "An Historical Study of a Racially Segregated School in New Jersey from 1886–1955" (Ed.D. diss., Rutgers University, 1984).

16. Wynetta Devore, "The Education of Blacks in New Jersey, 1900–1930: An Exploration in Oral History" (Ed. D. diss., Rutgers University, 1980).

17. Marion Thompson Wright, *The Education of Negroes in New Jersey* (New York: Bureau of Publications, Teachers College, 1941); Merle Curti was her dissertation advisor.

18. *Journal of Negro Education: Index to Volumes 1–31, 1932–1962* (Washington, DC: Howard University Press, 1962).

19. Jordan, *Reclaiming*.

20. This refers to presentations I've given at the New Jersey Historical Conference, Rowan College, November 3, 2017; the New Jersey State Library, Trenton, February 20, 2018; and the History of Education Society Annual Meeting, November 1, 2018. Also, Milagros Seraus-Roche, "Resisting Erasure: Reclaiming the Progressive Pedagogy and Practice of William Valentine," History of Education Annual Meeting, November 3, 2017. She also made presentations on Valentine and his wife Grace Valentine, an educator of distinction as well, at the 2018 HES meeting in Albuquerque.

21. Lawrence Cremin, *The Transformation of the School* (New York: Vintage Books, 1964), 28–9.

22. The 1913 article was later published as "Some Dangers in the Present Movement for Industrial Education," in *American Teacher* 2 (1913): 2–4; also *Middle Works*, Vol. 7: 98–103. The other, "A Policy of Industrial Education," *The New Republic*, December 19, 1914, 11–12; also *Middle Works*, Vol. 8: 97.

23. John Dewey, "Industrial Education – the Wrong Kind," *The New Republic* 2 (1915): 71–3; Dewey and David Snedden, "Two Communications," *The New Republic* (May 15, 1915): 40–44.

24. Thomas Jesse Jones, *Negro Education: A Study of the Private and Higher Schools for Negroes,* 2 vols. (Washington, DC: Government Printing Office, 1917); W.E.B. Du Bois, "Negro Education," *The Crisis* 15 (February 1918), 175–178.

25. Dewey refers to such segregation in "An Undemocratic Proposal" and in his dispute with Snedden; it's also discussed in *Democracy and Education* (New York: The Free Press, 1966/1916).

26. Thomas Fallace, *Dewey and the Dilemma of Race: An Intellectual History 1895–1922* (New York: Teachers College Press, 2012). A recent article that further examines Dewey's understanding of race is Kelly Vaughan, "Progressive Education and Racial Justice: Examining the Work of John Dewey," *Education and Culture* 34, no. 2 (2018): 39–68.

27. Menand, Louis *The Metaphysical Club: A Story of Ideas in America* (New York: Farrar, Straus and Giroux, 2001); see particularly chap. 14, "Pluralisms," 377–408.

28. Jordan, *Reclaiming*, 81–84. Some recent research by a new group in Bordentown called Building Bridges is uncovering the history of School No. 2, a segregated institution for black children that existed from the mid-1840s, initially as a private school, until 1948. In the spring of 2019, an exhibit and series of programs about School No. 2 and the Manual Training and Industrial School was presented by the Bordentown Historical Society. See https://bordentownhistory.org.

29. Ibid., 3–8. The estate had belonged to the family of the commander of the 1812 warship U.S.S. Constitution, recalled as "Old Ironsides"; hence another name by which the school was known.

30. The school's early years are told in Wright, *Education*, 178–180; Rice, *Reclaiming*; and more extensively in Nan Pillsbury, "Application for Landmark Status for Manual Training and Industrial School," National Register of Historic Places, U.S. Department of the Interior, 1997. Information in it was taken from annual reports to the New Jersey State Board of Education. "Application" is available through the New Jersey State Library, Trenton; this will be abbreviated as NJSL in subsequent references.

31. A laudatory article about the school under Gregory's leadership is "School of Great Promise," *New York Age,* September 21, 1905, 2.

32. "J.M. Gregory Out of Bordentown School," *New York Age,* February 11, 1915.

33. The December 28, 1920, issue of the "Weekly Letter of The Manual Training and Industrial School" gives an account of this visit. NJSA.

34. Focusing on these two topics was common in vocational education courses nationwide, for both black students and white, at the time; see Katherine S. Newman and Hella Winston, *Reskilling America: Learning to Labor in the Twenty-First Century* (New York: Henry Holt & Company, 2016), 67. The federal Smith-Lever Act of 1914 also focused on agricultural education; see Herbert Kliebard, *Schooled to Work* (New York: Teachers College Press, 1999), 133.

35. MTIS "Weekly Letter."

36. James D. Anderson, in *The Education of Blacks in the South, 1860–1935* (Chapel Hill: University of North Carolina Press, 1988), points this out on page 76. However, many similarities between the Dewey and the Washington programs have been noted in Donald Generals, Jr., *Booker T. Washington: The Architect of Progressive Education* (Houston: Strategic Book Publishing, 2013). Also instructive on this topic is Anthony DeFalco's article, "Analysis of John Dewey's Notion of Occupations," *Education and Culture* 26, no. 1 (2010): 82–99.

37. Kendall was a highly regarded educator himself; see "Dr. Kendall and Dr. Thomas," *Journal of the National Education Association* 11 (February 1922): 66.

38. Comment made in *A Place Out of Time.* See note 13.

39. "Harvard Class of 1904: Twenty-fifth Anniversary Report" (Cambridge, MA: Plimpton Press, June 1929). Available through the Harvard University Archives.

40. Adams, in "Role and Function," 75. She also claims that he wrote a regular column for a Newark newspaper; however archivists at the Newark Public Library were not able to locate such a column when I visited there in September 2018.

41. "Harvard Class of 1904: Fiftieth Anniversary Report, June 1954" (Cambridge: Harvard University Printing Office, 1954). Available through the Harvard University Archives.

42. Two of the most thorough histories of the school are the Pillsbury "Application for Landmark Status," 1997, and a 1936 Chronology in "Manual Training in Fiftieth Year of Growth and Progress," Press Service of the Bordentown School; available at NJSA, SEDMA01, Box 1. See also, Connie Goddard, "The Bordentown School as Institution and Idea," *New Jersey Studies: An Interdisciplinary Journal,* Summer 2018. https://njs.libraries.rutgers.edu/index.php/njs/article /view/125.

43. A romanticized illustration of the campus circa 1930 was commissioned in 1997 by John Medley, a 1954 graduate and archivist for the school.

44. "A Decade of Progress," published by the Manual Training School Extension Department, 1926. Unpaginated. NJSA.

45. Seinfel, "N.J. Negro School." See note 11.

46. The school's *Bulletin[s] of Information* issued in 1941 and 1943 offer the most extensive overview of the school and its programs. NJSA for 1941 bulletin; NJSL for 1943 bulletin.

47. Adams, "Role and Function," 88–94. See note 15.

48. The Memorial Day event is covered most vividly, using historical film footage, in *A Place Out of Time.* See note 13.

49. "New Jersey Manual Training School Pictorial Bulletin," produced by the school, 1940, NJSL.

50. Adams, "Role and Function," 63–67; Duck, "Historical Study," 105.

51. Arthur Symes in *A Place Out of Time;* an architect and eventually a college dean; in retirement, Symes took up sculpture.

52. Fallace's comments about the Deweys' description of the Indianapolis school also suggest a bit of "presentism" – given the realities black communities and educators faced at the time, what else might Valentine have done?

53. Dewey, "Learning to Earn."

54. A valuable contemporary analysis of Dewey's article is Anthony DeFalco, "Dewey and Vocational Education: Still Timely?" *Journal of School and Society* 3, no. 1 (2016): 54–64. In his "Address to National Negro Conference" (which had been organized by Du Bois), Dewey addressed racism in a manner that can be read as disputing some of Margonis's arguments; the address is in *Middle Works,* Vol. 4, 156–57.

55. Dewey, "Learning to Earn"; Dewey's comments, unless otherwise indicated, are from this article.

56. Though there is limited printed material to support this assertion, the graduates interviewed for *A Place Out of Time* certainly support it. See Symes "A Reflection on Bordentown" in 2016, described in note 12. Symes, Mildred Jordan, and others involved with the school spoke about its goals at a presentation organized by the New Jersey Institute for Social Justice, held in Mt. Holly, NJ, February 13, 2018.

57. Wright, *Education*, 183–88.

58. Devore, "Education of Blacks," 76–99.

59. MTIS. "A Decade of Progress"; Seinfel, "N.J. Negro School."

60. 1936 Chronology in "Manual Training in Fiftieth Year," 10–12. See note 42.

61. "Some Results of Bordentown Training," MTIS Extension Department, 1926. NJSA.

62. After 1945, when New Jersey began to harness discriminatory practices, opportunities for its black residents expanded. See Davidson M. Douglas, *Jim Crow Moves North: The Battle Over Northern School Segregation, 1865–1954* (New York: Cambridge University Press, 2005), 106, 183.

63. Career aspirations collected from *Echoes*, the annual yearbooks of the school; available in the State Archives, SEDMA01.

64. "Bulletin of Information," 1943, 10.

65. Barbara Wheeler, a 1953 graduate, asserted in the *Place Out of Time* video that MTIS students had no self-esteem issues. "They built us up," she claimed in the video.

66. Wheeler in *A Place Out of Time*. Activities are also described in the "Bulletin of Information," 1943, page 6; a scanned copy is available through the State Library in Trenton.

67. Another MTIS graduate reported in *A Place Out of Time* that the faculty did push them, but students knew the teachers weren't giving them a hard time just because they were black.

68. Typescript, Manual Training School, NJSA.

69. Wright, *Education*, 189.

70. Alridge, "Du Boisian Philosophy," 367.

71. Ibid., 370.

72. Students quoted in *A Place Out of Time* repeatedly assert this.

73. "Pictorial Bulletin," NJSL

74. Alridge, "Conceptualizing a Du Boisian Philosophy," 373.

75. Ibid., 359.

76. Pillsbury, "Application," 6–9.

77. Alridge, "Conceptualizing a Du Boisian Philosophy," 373.

78. Alridge cites a prescient forecast of opportunities for both blacks and whites, given as a 1930 graduation address at Howard University; see W.E.B Du Bois, "Education and Work," *Journal of Negro Education* 1, no. 1 (April 1932). A 1939

article written by Valentine's son echoes some of Du Bois's concerns; see William R. Valentine, Jr., "Bordentown Prepares for Industry," *Opportunity: The Journal of Negro Life* XVII, 1: 11–14.

79. Alridge, "Conceptualizing a Du Boisian Philosophy," 374–75.

80. The story of Dunbar is told in Alison Stewart, *First Class: The Legacy of Dunbar, America's First Black Public High School* (Chicago: Chicago Review Press, 2011). Two other books important to understanding secondary education for African Americans during this era are Craig Kridel, *Progressive Education in Black High Schools: The Secondary Schools Study, 1940–1946* (Columbia, SC: Museum of Education, University of South Carolina, 2015) and John L. Rury and Shirley A. Hill, *The African-American Struggle for Secondary Education: Closing the Graduation Gap* (New York: Teachers College Press, 2012).

81. James Anderson quotes sociologist Ralph Bullock and educator Benjamin Mays as making this claim. See his "Black Vocational Education" in Harvey–Tyack, eds., *Work, Youth, and Schooling* (Palo Alto: Stanford University Press, 1982), 201.

82. Adams, "Role and Function," 139–44. A stimulating account of the school's closing is Burkholder, "'Integrated Out of Existence'" see note 7.

83. George Streator, "School in Jersey Aids Negro Youths," published November 14, 1948. The article is available through the Harvard University Archives; the latter stamped it Washington, DC, *Star*, but the byline indicates it appeared in the *New York Times*.

84. W. R. Valentine, "Statement of Philosophy," typescript dated 10 December 1948; NJSA, SEDMA01, Box 1.

85. Jordan, *Reclaiming,* 92. Valentine died in 1954, after moving to New York City. An obituary appeared in the *New York Times*, November 3, 1954; a copy is available from the Harvard University Archives.

86. These were the students interviewed for *A Place Out of Time.*

87. Typescript of a Public Hearing before a commission established to . . . investigate . . . the proposed closing of the Bordentown Manual Training School, State House, Trenton, May 19, 1955, NJSL. A proposal to reopen the school is circulating among interested groups in New Jersey; see Andrea McChristian, *Bring Our Children Home: A Prison-to-School Pipeline* (Newark: Institute for Social Justice, published online, February 2018).

88. "Meyner in Dispute over Negro School," *New York Times,* June 3, 1955, 11. Available through ProQuest.

89. Constance Goddard, "Ella Flagg Young's Intellectual Legacy: Theory and Practice in Chicago's Schools. 1862–1917" (Ph.D. diss., University of Illinois at Chicago, 2005). As a graduate student, I also wrote about Young's intellectual relationship with both Du Bois and Booker T. Washington; "Democratic Schools for an Isolated Community: Interactions Among the Educational Programs of Ella Flagg Democratic Schools for an Isolated Community: Interactions Among

the Educational Programs of Ella Flagg Young, Booker T. Washington, and W.E.B. Du Bois," unpublished paper, summer 2003.

90. John T. McManis, *Ella Flagg Young and a Half Century of the Chicago Public Schools* (Chicago: A.C. McClurg, 1916); see esp. chapter 12, "Making Over a City School System," 175–199.

91. Ella Flagg Young, *Isolation in the School* (Chicago: University of Chicago Press, 1901), 101.

92. "Mrs. Ella Flagg Young Opposes 'Jim Crow' Schools"; headline in the *Chicago Defender*, Dec. 28, 1912, qtd. in Jackie M. Blount, "Individuality, Freedom, and Community: Ella Flagg Young's Quest for Teacher Empowerment," *History of Education Quarterly* 58, no. 2 (May 2018), note 75.

Bibliographty

The most extensive group of records about the Manual Training and Industrial School (MTIS) is located at the New Jersey State Archives in Trenton (some are also available in Special Collections, Rutgers University Library, New Brunswick). Those referred to in this paper are all at the State Archives, SEDMA01, Box 1; this is abbreviated as NJSA. All of these publications are listed below under Manual Training and Industrial School. References to John Dewey's articles are given both to their original publication and to a specific volume of *Middle Works* in the collection edited by Jo Ann Boydston, published by Southern Illinois University Press.

Adams, Ezola Bolden. "The Role and Function of the Manual Training and Industrial School at Bordentown as an Alternative School, 1915–1955." EdD. diss., Rutgers University, 1977.

Alridge, Derrick P. "Conceptualizing a Du Boisean Philosophy of Education: Toward a Model for African-American Education." *Educational Theory* 49, no. 3 (Summer 1999): 359–379.

———. *The Educational Thought of W.E.B. Du Bois: An Intellectual History.* New York: Teachers College Press, 2008.

Anderson, James D. *The Education of Blacks in the South, 1860–1935.* Chapel Hill: University of North Carolina Press, 1988.

Blount, Jackie M. "Individuality, Freedom, and Community: Ella Flagg Young's Quest for Teacher Empowerment." *History of Education Quarterly* 58, no. 2 (May 2018): 175–98.

Burkholder, Zoë. "'Integrated Out of Existence': African American Debates over School Integration versus Separation at the Bordentown School in New Jersey, 1886–1955," *Journal of Social History*, Fall 2017.

Cremin, Lawrence. *The Transformation of the School.* New York: Vintage Books, 1964.

Davidson, Dave, dir. *A Place Out of Time: The Bordentown School.* 2009; Bethel, CT: Hudson West Productions, DVD.

DeFalco, Anthony. "Analysis of John Dewey's Notion of Occupations," *Education and Culture* 26, no. 1 (2010): 82–99.

———. "Dewey and Vocational Education: Still Timely?" *Journal of School and Society* 3, no. 1 (2016): 54–64.

Devore, Wynetta. "The Education of Blacks in New Jersey, 1900–1930: An Exploration in Oral History." EdD. diss., Rutgers University, 1980.

Dewey, John. "Address to the National Negro Congress." 1909, *Middle Works*, Vol. 4, 156–57.

———. "Some Dangers in the Present Movement for Industrial Education." *American Teacher* 2 (1913): 2–4. (*Middle Works*, Vol. 7: 98–103).

———. "Learning to Earn: The Place of Vocational Education in a Comprehensive Scheme of Public Education." *School and Society* 5, no. 117 (March 24, 1917): 331–35.

———. "A Policy of Industrial Education." *The New Republic*, December 19, 1914, 11–12 (*Middle Works,* Vol. 8: 97).

———. "Industrial Education—A Wrong Kind," *The New Republic* 2 (1915): 71–73; and with David Snedden, "Two Communications," *The New Republic*, May 15, 1915, 40–44 (*Middle Works*, Vol. 8: 118–22).

———. *Democracy and Education.* New York: The Free Press, 1966/1916.

Dewey, John, and Evelyn Dewey. *Schools of Tomorrow.* Introduction by William W. Brickman. New York: E.P. Dutton & Co., 1962.

Douglas, Davidson M. *Jim Crow Moves North: The Battle Over Northern School Segregation, 1865–1954.* New York: Cambridge University Press, 2005.

"Dr. Kendall and Dr. Thomas." *Journal of the National Education Association* 11, (February 1922): 66.

Du Bois, W.E.B., Papers, Special Collections and University Archives, University of Massachusetts, Amherst, Libraries.

———. *The Souls of Black Folk.* New York: Bantam Books, 1989/1903.

———. "Negro Education: A Review." *The Crisis* 15, no. 4 (February 1918), 173-178.

———. "Education and Work." *Journal of Negro Education* 1, no. 1 (April 1932), 60-74.

Duck, Evelyn Blackmore. "An Historical Study of a Racially Segregated School in New Jersey from 1886–1955." EdD. diss., Rutgers University, 1984.

Fallace, Thomas. *Dewey and the Dilemma of Race: An Intellectual History, 1895–1992.* New York: Teachers College Press, 2011.

Generals, Donald, Jr. *Booker T. Washington: The Architect of Progressive Education.* Houston: Strategic Book Publishing, 2013.

Goddard, Connie, "The Bordentown School as Institution and Idea," *New Jersey Studies: An Interdisciplinary Journal,* Summer 2018. https://njs.libraries.rutgers.edu/index.php/njs/article/view/125.

————. "Ella Flagg Young's Intellectual Legacy: Theory and Practice in Chicago's Schools. 1862–1917." Ph.D. diss., University of Illinois at Chicago, 2005.

"Harvard Class of 1904. Twentieth Anniversary Report," June 1929, "Fiftieth Anniversary Report, June 1954" (Cambridge: Harvard University Printing Office, 1954). Available from the Harvard University Archives.

Jones, Thomas Jesse. *Negro Education: A Study of the Private and Higher Schools for Negroes*, 2 vols. Washington, DC: Government Printing Office, 1917.

Jordan, Mildred L. Rice. *Reclaiming African-American Students: Legacies, Lessons, and Prescriptions, The Bordentown School Model.* (Bloomington, IN: iUniverse, 2017).

Journal of Negro Education Index to Volumes 1–31, 1932–1962 (Washington, DC: Howard University Press, 1962).

Kantor, Harvey, and David Tyack, eds. *Work, Youth, and Schooling: Historical Perspectives on Vocationalism in American Education.* Palo Alto: Stanford University Press, 1982. See especially James. D. Anderson, "Black Vocational Education."

Kliebard, Herbert. *Schooled to Work: Vocationalism and the American Curriculum, 1876–1946.* New York: Teachers College Press, 1999.

Kridel, Craig. *Progressive Education in Black High Schools: The Secondary School Study, 1940–1946* Columbia, SC: Museum of Education, University of South Carolina, 2015.

Lewis, David Levering. *W.E.B. Du Bois: Biography of a Race, 1868–1919.* New York: Henry Holt & Company, 1993.

Manual Training and Industrial School (MTIS), Bordentown, NJ. "Weekly Letter of The Manual Training and Industrial School," December 28, 1920.

————. "A Decade of Progress." Unpaginated booklet, 1926.

————. "Some Results of Bordentown Training," 1926.

————. "Bordentown Manual Training School in Fiftieth Year of Growth and Progress," A Chronology. Typescript, 1936 or 1937 (conflicting information as to date).

————. "Pictorial Bulletin." 1940. (Scanned copy also available through the State Library, Trenton.)

————. *Bulletin of Information.* 1941.

————. *Bulletin of Information.* 1943, 10. (Scanned copy also available through the State Library, Trenton.)

————. *Echoes.* Annual Yearbooks of the Manual Training School, 1953, 1954, 1955.

Margonis, Frank. "John Dewey's Racialized Visions of the Students and Classroom Community," *Educational Theory* 59, no. 1 (2009): 17–39.

McChristian, Andrea. *Bring Our Children Home: A Prison-to-School Pipeline.* Newark: New Jersey Institute for Social Justice, published online, February 2018.

McManis, John. *Ella Flagg Young and a Half-Century of the Chicago Public Schools.* Chicago: A.C. McClurg, 1916.

Menand, Louis. *The Metaphysical Club: A Story of Ideas in America*. New York: Farrar, Straus and Giroux, 2001.

"Meyner in Dispute over Negro School." *New York Times,* June 3, 1955. Available through ProQuest.

New York Age. "School of Great Promise," September 21, 1905.

———. "J.M. Gregory Out of Bordentown School," February 11, 1915.

———. "Du Bois Speaks at Bordentown," August 18, 1922.

Rury, John L., and Shirley A. Hill. *The African-American Struggle for Secondary Schooling, 1940-1980: Closing the Graduation Gap*. New York: Teachers College Press, 2012.

Seinfel, Ruth. "N.J. Negro School." *New York Evening Post*, December 30, 1930. (Available at NJSA.)

Seraus-Roche, Milagros. "Resisting Erasure: Reclaiming the Progressive Pedagogy and Practice of William Valentine." Paper presented at the Annual Meeting of the History of Education Society, Little Rock, AR, November 3, 2017.

Stewart, Alison. *First Class: The Legacy of Dunbar, America's First Black Public High School*. Chicago: Chicago Review Press, 2011.

Streator, George. "School in Jersey Aids Negro Youths," November 14, 1948. (Available through the Harvard University Archives; though stamped by the archives Washington, DC, *Star*, byline credits the *New York Times*.)

Symes, Arthur. "A Reflection on Bordentown," *Diversity* (May 13, 2016), http://discovernjhistory.org/nj-blog/.

Tyack, David. *One Best System: A History of American Urban Education*. Cambridge: Harvard University Press, 1974).

Valentine, W. R. "Statement of Philosophy," Typescript, December 10, 1948. NJSA.

Valentine, William R., Jr. "Bordentown Prepares for Industry," *Opportunity: The Journal of Negro Life* XVII, no. 1 (1939): 1–14.

Vaughan, Kelly. "Progressive Education and Racial Justice: Examining the Work of John Dewey." *Education and Culture* 34, no. 2 (2018): 39–68.

"William R. Valentine." *New York Times,* November 3, 1954. Obituary available from the Harvard University Archives.

Wright, Marion Thompson. *The Education of Negroes in New Jersey*. New York: Bureau of Publications, Teachers College, Columbia University, 1941.

Young, Ella Flagg. *Isolation in the School*. Chicago: University of Chicago Press, 1901.

Connie Goddard, PhD, is a journalist and independent scholar who has taught at schools, colleges, and prisons in Chicago, New Jersey, and Romania. She is developing a website about Deweyan learning by doing and can be contacted at cg@conniegoddard.com.

Dewey's Ideas in Action! Continuing Professional Development in an International Community of Practice

Sabrina R. Goldberg

Abstract

Drawing on Dewey's concepts and thinking, a middle school mathematics teacher at The School at Columbia University describes her teaching practice and role as a field-based teacher-educator and professional development leader during EdTech Summit Africa. Through a first-person account of her experiences in Cape Town, Johannesburg, and Pretoria, South Africa, the author reflects on how professional development with technology was embraced and illuminates why the development of an international community of practice with primary, secondary, and tertiary teachers is evolving. The article is divided into four sections.

In the first section, the author relates how laboratory schools and communities of practice are no longer limited to a single geographic location and how boundaries for professional development are disappearing because of information and computer technology, such as the Internet, the World Wide Web, and globalization. The second section provides a narrative account of the professional development workshop experiences that occurred during EdTech Summit Africa 2017. In the third section, the author reflects on the conditions that she encountered in South Africa while leading professional development workshops on project-based learning and technology integration. This narrative underscores the importance of teacher training, continued professional development, communication and intercommunication between educators, and highlight the benefits of participating in a Professional Learning Network. The fourth section summarizes the value of collaboration among educators and the necessity for collective problem solving given extant research on the digital divide in South Africa.[1] Implications for educators are summarized and next steps for living Dewey's ideas in action are outlined.

Introduction

John Dewey's philosophy of education is ubiquitous. A prolific writer, educator, and philosopher of the 19th and 20th centuries, Dewey's educational philosophy resonates in the 21st century because he was a broadminded pragmatist who believed that "public education would sustain democratic ideals."[2] The corpus of his work, including founding the first Laboratory School at the University of Chicago in 1938,[3] prompted an array of public and private university affiliated laboratory schools to proliferate.[4] Since then, university-affiliated lab schools have served as sites for (1) research, experimentation, and development of child-centered and constructivist curriculum; (2) observation of child development theories and teacher-student interactions, and (3) preparation for pre-service teachers enrolled in university-affiliated teaching programs.[5] Overall, university-affiliated lab schools are regarded as demonstration schools for best practices and valued as "centers for teacher training and professional development."[6] More importantly, laboratory schools have taken on a community focus,[7] and this is significant because the term *community* is contextually bound.

Since Dewey wrote *Democracy and Education*[8] and *The Public and Its Problems*[9] technology has exploded exponentially, and his thinking on how we as individuals might transcend physical boundaries and become a "Great Community" (*The Public and Its Problems*, p. 170) remains prescient because conditions for communication and intercommunication have changed dramatically. Teachers may use technology to improve instructional delivery, integrate technology into their practice, and as a tool to problem solve and grow professionally. Teachers can rely on a variety of platforms, applications, digital networks, and professional communities for insights and advice. On the other hand, access to information and computer technology is not equitable.[10] In the absence of equitable access to technology, initiatives to support the development of international communities of practice have evolved.

Traditionally, a school's community referred to its geographic location, its students and their families, and society. Increasingly, however, the concept of community has expanded. It may apply to the neighborhood a lab school serves, such as the University of Pennsylvania's Sadie Alexander School,[11] which is a public school in West Philadelphia. Alternatively, The School at Columbia University (TSC), which is lab school affiliated with Columbia University (CU) serves the neighborhood surrounding CU.[12]

I teach Pre-algebra to seventh-graders at The School at Columbia University (TSC). As part of the mission and admissions policies, TSC employs half of my students' parents. The other half of my students live in the surrounding public-school districts and are admitted through a need-blind lottery process. This is significant since researchers note that Dewey talked about the importance of "community schools"[13] and how they might be utilized to provide opportunities for lifelong learning and civic participation. However, Dewey did not offer a specific formula for achieving these goals. Instead, community schools have become a participatory movement dependent on their stakeholders, including teacher-educators.

Beyond a public or private school identity and neighborhood served within a lab school setting, teacher-educators practice pedagogy that they have developed and feel passionate about utilizing. Wenger describes "groups of people who share a concern or a passion for something they do and learn how to do it better as they regularly interact" as *communities of practice*.[14] This phrase highlights a kinship and an identity of cooperation among teacher-educators who share educational methods and skills with fellow educators. The notion of communities of practice applies to continuing professional development as well.

Steyn described continuing professional development as a phenomenon in which "people engage in the process of collective learning in a shared domain of human endeavor and acquire knowledge and skills shared through joint activities and discussions."[15] According to Wenger,[16] the concept of communities of practice is not new. However, it is a concept that coheres with the current "international movement," in which university-affiliated educators engage in "growing international networks" sharing knowledge, research, educational expertise, disseminating instructional practices, and continuing professional development.[17]

Likewise, online professional communities can serve as sources for professional learning and reflection. Haythornthwaite and De Laat[18] found that network learning is usually about matters that teachers encounter directly in their work. Online communities link teachers to professional development networks (PLN) that help them to connect and "create structures on which learning opportunities can arise."[19] This expanded view of community and professional development[20] supports the supposition that Dewey's work resonates with 21st-century conceptions of democracy, educational reform,[21] and globalization.[22]

Drawing on John Dewey's work, I reflect below on my experience as a teacher-educator at TSC and professional development workshop presenter in South Africa. I describe personal insights on the benefits of joining a professional learning network (PLN) that provides professional development and international educational partnership opportunities. Based on this experience, I offer suggestions and outline next steps for educators who are interested in living Dewey's ideas in action.

EdTech Summit Africa 2017

According to Karen Page, founder of EdTech Summit Africa (ETSA), this organization is "an innovative teaching conference shared across Africa free of charge."[23] Founded, organized, and led by Karen Kirsch Page in 2012, ETSA is a Professional Learning Network (PLN). Teachers who join this network become members of a collaborative learning community (CLC) and remain connected digitally. The purpose of ETSA is to engage teachers as learners in a variety of best practices so that they can improve student achievement and classroom engagement. Workshop presenters share technological resources and teaching strategies that are grounded in experiential and self-directed learning theory.

I joined ETSA in South Africa from July 27–August 7, 2017 because it was an opportunity to collaborate with a diverse group of educators. I was prepared to share my practice so that South African teachers could potentially adopt or modify methods and teaching techniques that I developed. Moreover, I was curious about our intended audience, their culture, and their teaching experiences. Mostly, I was thrilled about the prospect of engaging with South African academics, secondary and tertiary teachers, pre-service teachers, and fellow travelers.

I imagined that this would be a worthwhile experience because I had previously collaborated with New York City public school teachers on the Millennium Cities Initiative (MCI), part of a three-year project led by the Earth Institute at Columbia University to attain Millennium Development Goals (MDG's) by the year 2015. Each of us was paired with teachers in Ghana through the School2School (S2S) initiative at Teachers College, Columbia University. Paired with three secondary mathematics teachers in Kumasi, our challenge was to create a team experience in a situation where access to the Internet and electricity was unreliable. Though I did not travel to Ghana, it was an empowering experience because we overcame these challenges. We relied on iEarn and digital technology, such as Google Classroom and Survey Monkey, to share information, lessons, and data that our students culled on the United Nations (UN) Millennium Development Goals (MDG's). Students compared goals that they believed were most important and achievable and used data to make predictions using the line of best fit. So when the opportunity to volunteer in South Africa arose, I imagined that collaborating face-to-face would be ideal because free communication had been the missing link. I wondered what South African teachers' experiences with technology were like, as well as their perceptions of technology integration. Overall, I looked forward to intercultural dialogue and what I could learn from this experience: how it might benefit my practice as a 7th-grade mathematics teacher at TSC, help me become a more reflective, culturally competent workshop presenter, and serve as a catalyst for continued active inquiry.

Self-directed and Experiential Learning

The ETSA presentation team included American and South African teacher-educators who were willing to share diverse skills, experience, and knowledge with other education professionals in hands-on interactive workshops designed to engage teachers and broaden understanding of what is possible in the classroom today. Several presenters had volunteered previously and were repeating in their roles as workshop leaders. Their commitment reinforced my desire to join ETSA.

My workshop, entitled "Visions of Possibility: Ignite student's imaginations about roles that they can play in their learning through flipped-teaching and project-based learning," highlighted the emphasis that I put on student autonomy in my practice. What I planned to talk about was how I motivate students to "mathematize"[24] and engage in social mathematics activities. I also planned to share a few short videos and iMovies that my students had crafted. These artifacts documented students engaged in "flipped teaching,"[25] demonstrated student ownership of algebraic concepts that they had mastered, and elements of selected mathematics projects, such as the Great Mathematician Project,[26] to serve as a springboard for discussion about oral, written, and digital skills that I assessed. In turn, workshop participants would be challenged to deconstruct what they saw and work collaboratively to identify skills that I evaluated.

For example, one of my students created an iMovie to illustrate how to solve an equation with variables on both sides. Using Keynote, a presentation software application, and auto shapes, he built multicolored boxes with different parts of the equation. Also, title cards were inserted using the Keynote animation feature and set to a timer to move every two seconds, then exported into an iMovie accompanied by relaxing electronic music. In contrast, other students created videos using their laptop cameras and Giant Post Its to demonstrate operations with rational numbers. Alternatively, they used classroom whiteboards to illustrate mastery of a mathematical concept of their choice. Altogether, student work represented self-directed and experiential learning; critical elements of my practice that I feel most passionate about and that demonstrate how I have structured my practice to empower 7th-grade students at TSC who are not grouped by ability.

I believed this non-traditional approach to learning would be compelling and thought-provoking because I had experience leading workshops on project-based learning through Teach 21: The Institute for 21st Century Teaching at TSC. Teach 21 offers workshops on how teachers at TSC develop authentic practices in academic instruction, project-based learning, inquiry, integrated curriculum, social justice and STEAM collaborations for teachers in public and private sector locally, nationally, and abroad. Thus I was accustomed to workshop participants from a range of public and private schools in urban, suburban, and rural sectors who had access to technology. One of my goals for ETSA was to challenge participants to think about how they would modify or adapt what they learned and brainstorm how they would implement it in their classrooms.

Toward that purpose, in preparation for ETSA I read research on teachers' perceptions of professional development workshops on technology integration,[27] and teachers' attitudes toward computer technology training,[28] and technology integration pedagogy.[29] Anyanwa[30] cited the importance of Web 2.0 tools in tailoring professional development workshops to have a positive impact on teachers, whereas Sabzian and Gilakjani[31] considered a full array of tech basics, from social media and tech integration to face-to-face integration with hands-on collaboration. Okijie, Olinzock and Okojie-Boulder[32] reported that teachers are not involved in technology decision-making, and that relevant objectives and methods of instruction are considered key to making a dynamic classroom. Given my teammates' biographic profiles and areas of expertise, I was confident that these themes would be addressed, and I was not disappointed.

I also read about continuing professional development (CPD) for teachers in general[33] and in South Africa, specifically.[34] Based on the results of 35 studies on professional development (PD) for teachers, Walters and Baffoe-Djan found seven aspects of PD that make the most difference to teachers:

> [PD that] is concrete and classroom-based, brings in expertise from outside the school; involves teachers in the choice of areas to develop and activities to undertake; enables teachers to work collaboratively with peers; provides opportunities for mentoring and coaching sustained over time; is supported by effective school leadership.[35]

Similarly, Mokhele and Jita conducted a six-year study on CPD. They found that "for CPD programs to be successful; they have to be personally meaningful to the participating teachers."[36] Steyn identified a key challenge for continuing professional development for teachers (CPD):

> encouraging a collaborative culture in communities of practice where teachers are involved in joint activities and discussions, assist one another and share knowledge and skills to improve the competence of teachers in South Africa.[37]

These findings on CPD for teachers piqued my curiosity. Though I had no preconceived notions about the communities of practice that I would encounter in South African township schools, I intended to share concrete examples of my practice, offering participants choice and activities for collaborative, hands-on work.

Reflective Thinking

Arriving in Cape Town, I was mesmerized by an endless landscape of South African township dwellings that lined the highway into Cape Town. As I stared, I recalled that I would be working with township teachers and visiting township schools. I understood our itinerary but didn't fully grasp these townships' historical, political, and economic significance. I did not know what townships looked like and I had not researched any of the locations that we were scheduled to visit—Langa, Khayelitsha, Alexandra, Diepsloot and Mamelodi. I learned firsthand that townships are considered relics of "apartheid planning" because they continue to function as isolated urban areas for non-whites.[38] From that point onward, the backdrop of Table Mountain and Signal Hill served as a dramatic counterpoint to township settlements and our lodging in the Sea Point district of Cape Town, where we gathered during the first week and bonded as a presentation team.

During days one and two we toured Langa, visited schools in Cape Town, and collaborated at the Bandwidth Barn in Khayelitsha, a township-technology hub. Throughout ETSA we toured township schools, described our workshops to teachers, and invited them to attend. We did not observe classroom instruction. We saw children dressed in uniforms, transitioning from one activity to another, joyfully playing outdoors, and interacted with confident middle school students who volunteered to give us tours of their school and answer our questions. We introduced ourselves to teachers during their breaks as they planned lessons, assessed, ate lunch, or surfed the Internet on cell phones.

As an inducement to attend our workshops, ESTA workshop presenters offered a short synopsis of the workshops we would lead. After a brief introduction, teachers received raffle tickets, and winners gleefully claimed gently used laptops and iPads donated to ETSA, as well as new thumb drives and ETSA tee shirts. Initially, offering raffle tickets and ETSA prizes seemed overzealous to me. Teachers' responses resembled a religious revival and I feared that we would be mistaken for technology evangelists. But once I realized that most teachers didn't have personal computers, a tool that I rely on routinely, I saw the value of this giveaway tactic for what it was; a core element of a purposeful design and an ingenious way to empower teachers for whom the cost of laptops and continuing professional development is prohibitive.

At the Bandwidth Barn in Khayelitsha, we strategized and tweaked our slide presentation decks. Work at the Bandwidth Barn stood out because we came together as a team, collaborated, and gave each other feedback, which I sorely needed after visiting the township schools that were surrounded by barbed wire, and either equipped with old computers or "missing computers" that were in need of repair or stolen. The impact of touring township schools was profound. The sheer density of township inhabitants was mindboggling. According to the World Bank, half of South Africa's urban population lives in townships, accounting for 38% of working-age citizens, but home to nearly 60% of its unemployed.[39]

Collaborating with the ETSA leadership team, I revamped my presentation at the Bandwidth Barn. I thought that teachers would benefit more from learning about Choice Theory,[40] and the alternative instructional methods that I use to differentiate and personalize student learning with learning menus, such as *Blendspace* (www.tes.com), to create interactive digital lessons and tiered assignments,[41] than a lecture on Dewey's view on the importance of activating imagination[42] or Maxine Greene's views on *Releasing the Imagination*,[43] as I had initially planned. I fully intended to share samples of my students engaged in flip teaching[44] and technology tools for project-based learning, such as *Inspiration* to create concept maps. I knew that I would discuss Connectivism, a digital learning theory,[45] but I wasn't confident about this approach, given the state of technology I saw during township school tours. Overall, the township tours reinforced my perception that teachers would benefit from more practical pedagogical methods and teaching techniques and not from lectures on theoretical approaches. Considering everything, I needed to strike a balance between content and teaching techniques, but there were so many options and not enough time to share more than one or two digital applications in depth. Consequently, I prepared a reading/resource list and was mentally prepared to improvise.

The presentation teams' task was to provide continuing professional development workshops that featured best practices and technology integration. Our audience included academic and tertiary faculty of the University of Cape Town (UCT), University of the Western Cape (UWC), Cape Peninsula of Technology (CPUT), and Stellenbosch University, at the Cape Teaching and Leadership Institute (CTLI) in partnership with the Education Technology Inquiry Laboratory (ETILAB). During the second week, we traveled to Johannesburg and stayed at a bed-and-breakfast in Melville that was surrounded by a wall topped with barbed wires. By day we visited LEAP 4 Science and Math High School in Diepsloot, a northern township, and presented for 90 teachers from LEAP 4, LEAP 3 located in Linbro Park, which serves the community of Alexandra, as well as neighboring Akani School in what was called an Ed Tech Summit "Pop Up."

The "Pop Up" featured light and quick versions of our workshops to be held at the University of Pretoria (UP) Mamelodi Campus on Saturday morning. This Summit was challenging because we were each given 15 minutes to present a compacted version of a 90-minute individual presentation, alongside two other colleagues, to a classroom of teachers. We transitioned after our collective 45-minute pitch to repeat our 3-way pitch in two additional rooms filled with teachers. This event was followed up on Saturday with our original 90-minute presentations for R-12 teachers at the University of Pretoria, Mamelodi Campus.

Travel Fellows

Another example of Dewey's ideas in action occurred through our work with travel fellows. As Dewey stated in *Democracy and Education*, "A democracy is more than a form of government; it is primarily a mode of associated living, of conjoint communicated experience."[46] A powerful example of associated living occurred through hands-on work in focused training sessions with our travel fellows.

In addition to workshop presentations, at the conclusion of our stay in Cape Town, and again in Johannesburg, we were tasked with leading two focused training sessions with our "travel fellows"—teachers from communities and schools who had previously attended an EdTech Summit or whose district would not be served by ETSA. The leadership team devised a national application process, which included all past Summit locations, to help build teacher leaders and empower them to take their experience back to their communities and share what they learned with other teachers.

Travel fellows lived with us, attended our workshops, and traveled with us. Though I did not think it was possible, collaborating with travel fellows to create slide presentations that they would share in their home communities rivaled my Summit experiences. Working with travel fellows was an intellectual exercise, an open-ended heuristic, exploratory in nature and experiential. Through this dynamic, I learned what the fellows learned and valued as participants in our workshops. However, they did so without computer skills or prior knowledge on how to create Google slides or PowerPoint presentations.

Choreographed like speed dating, for this event fellows rotated between pairs of workshop presenters for technical support. If I had the opportunity to do this over, I would have assigned fellowship travelers videos to watch, and challenged them to find instructional videos that they thought were more informative or engaging than the ones I suggested. Alternatively, I would have provided articles with diagrams on how to organize and craft slide decks. Even so, this activity was a highlight for me because I got to know everyone better—presenters and travel fellows.

Critical Reflection

In *How We Think* Dewey stated, "We do not learn from experience, we learn from reflecting on experience."[47] Dewey considered reflection "a meaning-making process, and a disciplined way of thinking, that needs to happen in a community in interaction with others and requires attitudes that value personal and intellectual growth of oneself and others"[48] Based on these four criteria, the following interactions with workshop participants stood out to me.

The first workshop, on Summit day one at CTLI in Cape Town, included university educators working with pre-service teachers. Even though there were technical glitches, participants were patient, and after an icebreaker activity introducing themselves to one another and the group at large, they readily engaged in watching the iMovie on solving equations with variables on both sides. Initiating discussion on assessment was difficult. So, I relied on teacher wait time. Participants were polite, yet pensive. They expressed an interest in watching another video, and I complied. Then a participant asked about the amount of time it took to make videos and iMovies, to which I responded that students were given 3 class periods, but had access to technology at home. That same participant, a graduate school English instructor, indicated that his students took two weeks to complete a similar task. I then segued into a discussion about how students at TSC have access to technology in grades K-8, and how we scaffold student work in each division collaboratively with the help of technology integrationists and learning specialists. This sequence of events led to a productive discussion on the value of alternative instructional approaches, such as flip teaching[49] and project-based learning. As I reflected on the trajectory of our discussions, I realized that we were becoming a community of practice[50] as we problem solved, and as I shared professional anecdotes and resources. It felt like innovation was doable because I was offering solutions and resources that could move change forward.

This discussion was qualitatively different from my workshop the following day, which was attended by pre-service teachers who had little experience with technology. Upon reflection, I realized that my concerns about Summit day one stemmed from the fact that I had not started a PD workshop with flip teaching before. I often start a workshop with Choice Theory[51] and segue into alternative instructional approaches that help personalize student learning. Though teachers were open to these nontraditional approaches and the idea of empowering students, I was perplexed by the silence I encountered until a participant raised the issue of standards, testing, and teaching constraints. I had access to K–12 standards in South Africa and related how they should start small, identifying one or two technology innovation goals.

Informed that they had little autonomy regarding the way they structured coursework, we talked about pacing and tiered assignments[52] in mixed-ability classrooms.[53] I explained that we do not group students by ability at TSC. To differentiate curriculum, I offer students a choice between "regular and spicy" mathematics homework assignments, so that students can self-identify, topic by topic, their comfort zones with specific content. Regular assignments cover content taught, and that is expected of all students to practice independently, whereas spicy assignments are more complex and offer challenging extensions. However, students' choices, "regular" or "spicy," are weighted equally.

Subsequently, during a discussion on assessments and testing, I explained that students were learning for mastery, not grades, and an opportunity to correct mistakes on quizzes was offered to all students, as was extra time to complete assessments. There was also an opportunity to retest, whether or not they qualified for special accommodations, because TSC is a progressive laboratory school and our focus is on "the individual child" as an emerging learner "rather than upon a traditional curriculum. . . . [Thus] we make schooling adaptive to the needs" of our students.[54]

As the session concluded, I felt that I had connected with my participants. This connection was evident when I shared *Blendspace* (www.tes.com), as a digital resource for differentiating lessons and organizing components of lessons or projects with digital resources (e.g., websites, videos, worksheets, games, and articles). The connection was also evident in the quality of our discussion, which was measured and thoughtful.

On Summit day two, critical reflection was triggered when I asked 24 participants to discuss with a partner the following icebreaker question: "Why did you become a teacher?" Despite the time limit they were given, participants were reluctant to stop talking. The theme of becoming a teacher out of necessity versus becoming a teacher out of genuine love for teaching and learning triggered emotions for many. In that moment, I reflected on how important it is for teachers to talk with one another and be given the opportunity to reflect, compare notes, and bond, as they explored lessons that I had crafted on *Blendspace* (www.tes.com) and were challenged to drag and drop resources for an experience of their choice with this software application. Participants also experimented with *Inspiration;* working in pairs, they were tasked with crafting concept maps showing how they connected.

On the last Summit day, the level of engagement and participation was high. At this session, teachers collaborated and shared professional challenges. One teacher shared her frustrations about teaching 52 second-grade students in one classroom, and the chaos that erupted when she showed a video. I offered some strategies, like collaborating with colleagues to implement technology integration rules and behavior expectations for students. I described flexible grouping strategies, such as station rotations with only one group of students at a time being allowed to view the video, and each student assigned a specific task within each group at each station. I also advised her to group students deliberately for academic and social-emotional reasons, and to experiment with showing a video to one group a day to ensure the control she wanted. It felt like I was reinforcing behaviorism, but she needed advice on how to integrate technology, direction on how to choreograph flexible grouping, student choice, and learning menus, and I think the entire group benefited from this discussion as well.

Another theme that teachers brought up was a lack of time to implement non-traditional instructional strategies, such as flipped-teaching and project-based learning with limited or no access to technology. A teacher-in-training talked about how his father, a goat farmer, had made sacrifices so that he could pursue a teaching career. When he described being an intern and how difficult it was to juggle a prescribed curriculum, as well as how defeated he felt knowing that his professor was dissatisfied with the very curriculum they were mandated to instruct, I empathized and shared relevant experiences and details about my educational background. I shared how I had experienced corporal punishment in grade school, failed algebra, the very subject I teach, but passed statistical regression analysis in graduate school, and now considered myself a work-in-progress—happiest when teaching or learning something new. Moreover, I shared how important it is to cultivate a growth mindset,[55] and promised to connect him with a professor in South Africa to counterbalance his current situation. I followed through on my pledge.

This Summit stood out because I was "reflecting in action" and "reflecting on action"[56]—offering teaching techniques that I had grappled with and solutions that worked in my practice. Additionally, I asked participants to note technology sources, so I made an adjustment that I felt proud of and was able to accomplish all that I planned, including a more extended question and answer session. As the workshop concluded, I reflected on my interview for ETSA.

Before arriving in South Africa, I was informed by Karen Kirsch Page that teachers might have no access or limited access to technology and asked what I would do. At the time, I said I would use storytelling to describe experiences where I overcame obstacles by taking baby steps, collaborating with colleagues, and prototyping innovations. Page also informed me that most teachers had cell phones with high data costs and pay-as-you-go plans, but none of this penetrated until I got to South Africa!

Although the impact of teaching with limited access to technology was powerful, seeing teachers using their cell phones was encouraging. As a result, I shared education sites and technology networks that they could access with cell phones to find solutions, build capacity, partner with other teachers to implement technology, and plan lessons or projects. I also used cell phones as a springboard for discussion on Connectivism[57] and global education networks that are accessible on their cell phones. I recommended specific resources, like *Edmodo, Edsurge, Edutopia, Edudemic, ISTE,* and *Mindshift,* to stay current on teaching strategies and technology innovation, and iEarn, as I had for the School to School (S2S) initiative, to connect with teachers on global learning projects. I was not sure how sustainable or cost-effective these suggestions were, but it seemed like a starting point for an open-ended discussion about "collaboration and engagement in a cycle of planning, action, reflection or evaluation."[58]

Democracy, Experience, and Education

Upon returning from South Africa, I reflected on my experience, wrote a blog post titled "Energized and transformed,"[59] and reread selected works by Dewey and about his legacy. I reflected on his philosophy and the timeliness of his ideas. Dewey was dedicated to the "theory and practice" of democracy,[60] and as his philosophy of education evolved, his conception of education democracy expanded. As a result, Dewey inspired generations of teacher-educators, like myself, to pick up where he left off: preparing teachers to "better people's quality of life" by sharing their "aims and methods,"[61] so that democracy is achievable. Toward that purpose, in an analysis of Dewey's work and its continuing relevance today, Gordon stated,

> Dewey's vision of democracy challenges us to recreate our global communities and our systems of education to meet the changing circumstances of history, so that all citizens of democratic societies imagine new ways of association and interaction that promote a respect for freedom, equality and diverse ways of being in the world.[62]

Likewise, in *Dewey's Dream: Universities and Democracies in an Age of Education Reform,* the authors explained how Dewey's vision of community schools had influenced an international movement that places civic responsibility on universities. [63] Hence, whether Dewey's ideas about democracy convey a vision[64] or a dream,[65] the "tensions and relationships among Dewey's ideas"[66] resonate with the idea that Dewey viewed democracy as a "participatory process"[67] that is dependent on teacher-educators. Significantly, Nebeker stated, "Dewey envisioned" that teachers "would be the axis upon which such a democracy revolved."[68]

Teacher Preparation, Globalization, and Continuing Professional Development

To cultivate and sustain a democracy, Dewey considered teacher preparation "essential."[69] He believed that teacher-educators should "foster dispositions and attitudes that cultivate curiosity, open-mindedness, and reflective and active inquiry."[70] Curiosity would reflect the teachers' desire to learn. Open-mindedness would speak to a teacher's capacity to grow, embrace diversity, and exhibit empathy, whereas reflective and active inquiry would manifest in the teacher's concerns and passions as a practitioner. These dispositions were essential to Dewey because he viewed democracy as much more than a political system.[71]

Dewey viewed democracy "as a personal way of life, a mode of associated living, and a moral ideal."[72] As he argued, "we need to get rid of the habit of thinking of democracy as something institutional and external and acquire the habit of treating it as a personal way of life."[73] In turn, this would require educators to "approach democracy experimentally, pluralistically and fallibly."[74] Dewey's rationale was simple. Experimentation provides educators with an opportunity to test ideas and see how well they work in practice. A commitment to pluralism shows that "shared interests among individuals and free interaction" are valued.[75] Moreover, when we as educators recognize our limitations, flawed thinking, and biases, our fallibility permits us to seek "ongoing ways to improve our ideas and ideals."[76] In sum, democracy requires "a disposition of openness, tolerance, and respect."[77]

Preparing teachers for the role they will play in society has been enhanced by digital technology and access to information. Since Dewey's death in 1952, digital technology has accelerated access to global teaching and learning. As noted by Gordon, globalization "has contributed to the accelerated circulation of goods, information, and people around the globe, and changed the shape of education through the increase in digital technologies mediating interactions between teachers and students."[78] Therefore, globalization has created new opportunities for international educational collaboration and education reforms that privilege student-centered learning. This bodes well for teacher-educators leading continuing professional development workshops, as we can share how our dispositions and attitudes have led us on a particular course of action or inquiry in our practice and can offer authentic responses to participants' queries, interests, and personal concerns. Moreover, as a result of globalization, the teachers' role in higher education can shift to "pedagogical approaches that foster imagination, empathy, and third voice."[79] According to English, the third voice has many benefits: It "productively mediates interactions between participants, including teacher and learners" and "serves to facilitate critical reflection within cross-cultural learning contexts,"[80] something I experienced firsthand.

Benefits of International Collaborative Learning Communities

As Dewey stated in *Democracy and Education*, "real learning occurs after an event when an experience is reconstructed."[81] Traveling to South Africa and subsequently writing and reconstructing this experience in narrative form resonates with his thinking about how real learning occurs. Similarly, in a review of *Dewey's Dream*, Saltmarsh stated, "education transforms the individual in such a way that what they know becomes who they are."[82]

Joining ETSA was an experiment and a personally meaningful new experience for me. Although I had presented workshops on project-based learning voluntarily, I had not traveled internationally and worked in a voluntary capacity as a teacher-educator. I learned a lot about myself: about how open-minded I am, about my tolerance for change, and my respect for others.[83] Nevertheless, it was an experience that contributed to my self-education; and when I left South Africa, I felt energized and transformed. What was energizing was connecting with South African educators, sharing insights on teaching students who are not grouped by ability, and anecdotes about how and why I developed my practice in a university-affiliated laboratory school that privileges social-emotional learning. What was transformative was the potential for community empowerment and professional collaboration among educators in a vast international learning community.

For example, collaborating with South African teachers and travel fellows was empowering. Participants gained knowledge from me and vice versa. Aside from developing a new perspective on global teaching and developing relationships with a cohort of teachers that I traveled, communed, and worked with, I shared a sense of purpose and felt connected to the presentation team. As we bonded, our kinship grew. This experience validated our beliefs about technology integration and, through this process, we became a community of collaborators. We also became a community of practice[84] as we shared insights on technology tools, discussed our interactions with workshop participants, and compared notes. When we were not in a professional mode, we embraced every opportunity to experience authentic South African art, food, Pinotage wine, music, and culture.

It was equally empowering to mediate interactions, facilitate critical reflection as English described, share resources with workshop participants, and help colleagues expand their skill set and potentially transform their practice. I left South Africa confident that I belonged to a global community of educators who are committed to our students and our profession. Moreover, I felt that sharing what I know, and helping fellow educators understand the powerful professional learning networks that operate in education and education technology, were worth pursuing.

Implications

While personal and professional benefits were realized by the author, there are significant implications for all educators. As noted by many,[85] teachers need to engage in professional development workshops with each other *and* with technology. They also need to learn how to use technology. Toward that goal, in the *Public and Its Problems*, Dewey stated, "We have the physical tools of communication as never before,"[86] and to a certain extent that is true. However, access to technology is not equitable.

Access to Professional Development with Technology

In the 21st century, information and computer technology have had a significant impact on the individual and collective identities of professional educators. Increased access to information on the World Wide Web and its networks underscores that there are fewer physical boundaries between educators in this era of globalization.[87] Dewey addressed factors that can remove boundaries and help people to connect. As he explained,

> Every expansive era in the history of mankind has coincided with the operation of factors which have tended to eliminate distance between peoples and classes previously hemmed off from one another . . . Travel, economics and commercial tendencies have at present gone far to break down external barriers, to bring peoples and classes into closer and more perceptible connections with one another.[88]

During ETSA, workshop leaders accessed information at the Bandwidth Barn in Khayelitsha and through personal devices, such as cell phones, laptops, and tablets. In this cross-cultural context, ESTA workshop presenters and participants transcended global barriers by working face-to-face and side-by-side on activities that were hands-on. Participants accessed computers in each of the computer labs in which workshops were conducted. Then participants used the technology at their fingertips to access information and complete a task. Workshop participants also used technology as a tool to explore technology integration resources, applications, and search engines that were identified during workshop presentations.

Under these conditions, access to technology united teachers who were intent on learning how to integrate technology into their practice. Access to the Internet also provided workshop participants with tips on how to leverage professional learning opportunities in the absence of working face-to-face interactions with workshop facilitators. Most importantly, professional development workshops with technology promoted "promising pedagogical discussions between educators."[89] The rationale for providing workshop participants with the opportunity to access information and use computer technology was to enhance future instruction and support project-based learning outcomes. In addition, participants learned how to use technology to connect with a global network of educators. In turn, this reinforced the notion that we, as educators, are all part of a larger international global community—one that is at the forefront in developing an international community of practice.

For example, identifying Professional Learning Networks (PLN's) helped teachers connect digitally and promoted teacher communication and intercommunication after ESTA concluded. These resources for educators provide continued professional development and international educational partnership opportunities. Overall, the promise of PLN's is their emphasis on teacher interdependence, collaboration, and communication. These factors foster teacher empowerment and enable educators to discuss their individual concerns and challenges informally. For instance, during ETSA educators discussed what is going on in their individual "communities of practice,"[90] and after ETSA participants contacted workshop presenters enquiring about topics of concern to them and their professional development, including graduate programs and fellowship opportunities in education technology.

Furthermore, during ESTA, teachers shared goals, objectives, and practices from their own personal perspectives. This is significant because, as Dewey asserted, "Any education given by a group tends to socialize its members, but the quality and value of the socialization depends upon the habits of the group."[91] As a result, the conditions under which communication and intercommunication between teachers takes place are key factors that support professional growth and foster a collective identity among educators.

From a "Great Society" to a "Great Community"

In *The Public and Its Problems*, Dewey explained why he considered a "Great Society" impersonal, and how it might become a "Great Community" that privileges personal and meaningful communication. Dewey reasoned, "The machine age in developing the 'Great Society' has invaded and partially disintegrated the small communities of former times without generating a 'Great Community.'"[92] Dewey wondered how the public would overcome this conundrum and surmised, "the solution is bound up with restoring a sense of communal life that can move us from an impersonal 'Great Society' into a personal and meaningful 'Great Community.'"[93]

Dewey argued that "a Great Community" is conceivable "in the sense of free and full intercommunication."[94] Toward that purpose, Dewey believed that technology would play a role in this transformation and help create a great community. In many ways, Dewey's vision of a "Great Community" was put into action by workshop presenters and participants during ETSA, as workshop presenters and travel fellows communed together and used a collaborative structure to communicate with each other. For instance, in addition to communing together we used *WhatsApp*, *GroupMe*, and *Flipgrid* cell phone applications to intercommunicate digitally. These observations resonate with Dewey's perspective on how knowledge is transmitted.

According to Dewey, "knowledge is a function of association and communication: it depends upon tradition, upon tools and methods socially transmitted, developed and sanctioned."[95] This was evident during ETSA when communication and intercommunication among educators were unlimited. However, according to Ghobadi and Ghobadi, "inequalities in the access to and use of information and communication technologies" have created "access gaps" and "shaped a digital divide."[96] Based on this premise, Ghobadi and Ghobadi identified four different access gaps for educators. These involved motivation, material, skills, and usage.

Though educators in attendance at ETSA exhibited "motivation to learn recent technology,"[97] had access to information and communication technologies materials (e.g., computers and cell phones), exposure to technology integration skills, and were provided with an opportunity to practice accessing information, a "lack of network infrastructure and electricity"[98] prevented township teachers from accessing the Internet and using computer resources. As Bornman pointed out, "compared with developed countries, as well as with developing countries, South Africa has lower individual Internet usage rates; lower computer ownership; and lower broadband subscription rates."[99] Similarly, Mashile conducted a study on factors that impact South African educators' ability to integrate technology in classrooms and found that "training and professional development were severely lacking and these two factors impact on educators' ability to integrate technology in South Africa."[100] According to Mashile "only 26% of educators in South Africa have basic information and communications technology (ICT) skills."[101]

The idea of a digital divide was pointedly reinforced during ETSA workshops by participants who communicated their frustrations with a lack of access to technology and, conversely, with integrating technology into a prescribed curriculum. The digital divide was also reinforced at the conclusion of each workshop program when participants convened to reflect on workshop experiences. During closing remarks, participants expressed how they benefitted from the workshops that they attended. Although some participants shared frustrations that they had accessing technology resources, others described how they had benefitted and planned to implement something new that they learned as a result of the ETSA professional development workshops they attended.

Next Steps

The conditions under which communication and intercommunication among educators' who commune, connect, and work together to develop international communities of practice in education is important. Documenting how we as teachers collaborate with one another in a global context is both relevant and timely. It supports the notion that Dewey's work resonates with 21st-century conceptions of democracy, educational reform,[102] and globalization.[103] But if we as educators want to personally experience the true meaning of democracy, which Dewey defined as "a life of free and enriching communion,"[104] we would all benefit from taking a more proactive stance.

According to Dewey, "the task of democracy is forever that of creation of a freer and more humane experience in which we all share and to which all contribute."[105] To embrace living Dewey's ideas in action, individual educators in our "Great Society" can use technology, as he stated, "to secure the intellectual and emotional significance of this physical annihilation of space,"[106] which the Internet and World Wide Web signify, to advance a more personal and meaningful "Great Community."

Fast forward to the 21st-century and the explosion of computerized technology. While the "development of tools into machines" was described by Dewey as "characteristic of the industrial age," he also stated that,

> It was made possible by taking advantage of science socially accumulated and transmitted . . . it was no natural endowment but something acquired by observing others, by instruction, and communication.[107]

Bearing this in mind, computerized machines used for technology information can be used as educational tools, but they are in no way a substitute for interactions and communication with educators who instruct and can be observed while instructing.

Educators who do not have access to personalized professional development workshops with technology can use social media to hone and expand their personal, interpersonal, and professional communication skills. By using social media tools and mobile applications, it is conceivable that individual educators in South Africa can overcome the digital divide described by Bornman, Ghobadi and Ghobadi, and Mashile. However, this will require a great deal of problem solving and, more specifically, joint "problem solving with new potential collaborators."[108]

In place of open access to digital educational resources, mobile phones can provide opportunities to access networked communication. Educators can collaborate and share information that they have accessed on their mobile phones. Social media tools and mobile applications, such as *YouTube, Instagram,* and *Twitter,* are currently very popular and potentially informative. This is significant because, according to Bornman, "ownership of mobile phones was much higher than the use of computers and the Internet in South Africa."[109] Bornman also noted that, "97.7% of teachers with tertiary qualifications in South Africa, reported that they used their own mobile phones to access Internet information."[110]

Alternatively, free technology hubs, like the Bandwidth Barn in Khayelitsha, can be used to access Professional Learning Networks (PLN) like Edmodo, Classroom 2.0, and The Educator's PLN.[111] These online sources function "as a system of interpersonal connections and resources that support informal learning."[112] As such, they can be used to connect with potential collaborators for advice, support, and to brainstorm solutions. Online professional development networks (PLN's) can help teachers to connect and "create structures on which learning opportunities can arise."[113] In sum, a key bonus for educators who engage in online communication is that they can communicate, collaborate, and problem solve informally.

In general, educators can use online PLN's to describe a concern or challenge. Through dialogue with other educators, in PLN's they can identify resources and continuing professional development opportunities, such as free sources for technology materials, including video tutorials on technology use and technology integration skills. Likewise, information on fellowships and grants for computer technology training can be identified and shared as well. Through communication and intercommunication, educators can problem solve together. This type of "collective problem solving"[114] will ultimately reinforce "a view that sees democracy as always a task before us, but as nonetheless containing the resources within itself to imagine beyond its specific limitations."[115]

Overall, though conditions for Internet access are very challenging in South Africa, professional development workshops and professional learning networks that privilege collaborative learning can help bridge the digital divide. But bridging the gap between "those who have and those who do not have access to new forms of technology information,"[116] and professional development with technology, will be a monumental task in South Africa unless "ongoing research, to monitor the impact of various initiatives,"[117] such as ETSA, is undertaken.

NOTES

1. Elirea Bornman, "Information Society and Digital Divide in South Africa: Results of Longitudinal Surveys," *Information, Communication & Society* 19, no. 2 (2016): 264–78. https://doi.org/10.1080/1369118X.2015.1065285; Shahla Ghobadi and Zahra Ghobadi, "How Access Gaps Interact and Shape the Digital Divide: A Cognitive Investigation," *Behaviour & Information Technology* 34, no. 4 (2015): 330–40, http://dx.doi.org/10.1080/0144929X.2013.833650; Thubelihlelenkululeko Zonke Mashile, *Technology and the Digital Divide: Understanding Factors that Impact on Educators' Ability to Integrate Technology in South African Classrooms* (Illovo: Gordon Institute of Business Science, University of Pretoria, 2016).

2. Melia L. Nebeker, "The Teacher and Society: John Dewey and the Experience of Teachers." *Education and Culture* XIX, no. 2 (Fall 2002): 19, https://www.jstor.org/stable/42922389.

3. Theodore Michael Christou, "21st- Century Learning, Educational Reform, and Tradition: Conceptualizing Professional Development in a Progressive Age," *Teacher Learning and Professional Development* 1, no. 1 (2016): 61–72, http://journals.sfu.ca/tlpd/index.php/tlpd/article/download/10/11; Maia Cucchiara, "New Goals, Familiar Challenges? A Brief History of University-Run Schools," in *Perspectives on Urban Education* (Summer 2010): 96–108, https://urbanedjournal.gse.upenn.edu/sites/default/files/pdf_archive/PUE-Summer2010-V7I1-pp96-108.pdf.

4. Christou, "21st- Century Learning."; Cucchiara, "New Goals, Familiar Challenges?"; Nebeker, "The Teacher and Society"; Sri Rachmajanti and Maureen McClure, "University-Affiliated Lab Schools: A Collaborative Partnership Between the University of Pittsburgh's Falk School, and the State University of Malang Lab Schools," *Excellence in Higher Education* 2, no. 1 (2011): 11–20, https://doi .org/10.5195/ehe.2011.40.

5. Cucchiara, "New Goals, Familiar Challenges"; Elizabeth Henning, Gadija Petker, and Nadine Petersen. "University-Affiliated Schools as Sites for Research Learning in Pre-Service Teacher Education," *South African Journal of Education* 35, no. 1 (2015): 1–8, https://doi.org/10.15700/201503070014.

6. Rachmajanti & McClure, "University-Affiliated Lab Schools," 12.

7. Lee Benson, John Puckett, and Ira Harkavay, *Dewey's Dream: Universities and Democracies in an Age of Education Reform, Civil Society, Public Schools, and Democratic Citizenship* (Philadelphia: Temple University Press, 2007); Cucchiara, "New Goals, Familiar Challenges"; Mordecai Gordon, "Why Should Scholars Keep Coming Back to John Dewey?" *Journal of Educational Philosophy* 48, no. 10 (2016): 1–15, https://doi.org/10.1080/00131857.2016.1150800.

8. John Dewey, *Democracy and Education. An Introduction to the Philosophy of Education* (New York: Macmillan Publishers, 1916).

9. John Dewey, (1927) 2016, *The Public and Its Problems: An Essay in Political Inquiry,* edited by Melvin L. Rogers (Athens: Ohio University Press).

10. Bornman, "Information Society and Digital Divide in South Africa"; Ghobadi and Ghobadi, "How Access Gaps Interact"; Thubelihlelenkululeko Zonke Mashile, *Technology and the Digital Divide: Understanding Factors that Impact on Educators' Ability to Integrate Technology in South African Classrooms* (Illovo: Gordon Institute of Business Science, University of Pretoria, 2016).

11. Cucchiara, "New Goals, Familiar Challenges," 101.

12. Cucchiara, "New Goals, Familiar Challenges"; Sarah D. Sparks, "Amid Changing Landscapes, Lab Schools Search for New Roles," in *Education Week*, February 24, 2015, https://www.edweek.org/ew/articles/2015/02/25/lab-schools -search-for-new-roles.html.

13. Benson, Puckett, and Harkavay, *Dewey's Dream*.

14. Etienne Wegner, "Communities of Practice. A Brief Introduction," (paper presented at the STEP Leadership Workshop, University of Oregon, OR, October 2011), 1, https://scholarsbank.uoregon.edu/xmlui/bitstream/handle/1794/11736/A%20 brief%20introduction%20to%20CoP.pdf?sequence=1&isAllowed=y.

15. G. M. Steyn, "Continuing Professional Development for Teachers in South Africa and Social Learning Systems: Conflicting Conceptual Frameworks of Learning," *Koers* 73, no. 1 (July 2008): 20, https://doi.org/10.4102/koers.v73i1.151.

16. Wenger, Etienne, *Communities of Practice: Learning, Meaning, and*

Identity. (Cambridge: Cambridge University Press, 1998), http://dx.doi.org/10.1017/CBO9780511803932.

17. Rachmajanti & McClure, "University-Affiliated Lab Schools," 12.

18. Caroline Haythornthwaite and Maarten DeLatt, "Social Networks and Learning Networks: Using Social Network Perspectives to Understand Learning," in *Proceedings of the 7ᵗʰ International Conference on Networked Learning,* edited by Lone Dirckinck-Holmfeld, Vivien Hodgson, Chris Jones, Maarten de Laat, David McConnell, and Thomas Ryberg, (Lancaster: Lancaster University, 2010), 183–90, https://www.lancaster.ac.uk/fss/organisations/netlc/past/nlc2010/abstracts/PDFs/Haythornwaite.pdf.

19. Maarten De Latt, *Enabling Professional Development Networks: How Connected Are You?* (Heerlen: Open University, 2012), 183.

20. Christou, "21st-Century Learning"; Catherine Walters and Jessica Briggs Baffoe-Djan, *What Professional Development Makes the Most Difference to Teachers?* (Oxford: Oxford University Press, 2012).

21. Benson, Puckett, and Harkavay, *Dewey's Dream*; Andrea R. English, "John Dewey and the Role of the Teacher in a Globalized World: Imagination, Empathy, and 'Third Voice,'" *Educational Philosophy and Theory* 48, no. 10 (2016): 1046–64, https://doi.org/10.1080/00131857.2016.1202806; Emil Višňovský and Štefan Zolcer, "Dewey's Participatory Educational Democracy," *Educational Theory* 66, no. 1–2 (2016): 55–71, https://doi.org/10.1111/edth.12152.

22. Gordon, "Why Should Scholars Keep Coming Back to John Dewey?"; Mordecai Gordon and Andrea R. English, "John Dewey's Democracy and Education in an Era of Globalization," *Educational Philosophy* 48, no. 10 (2016): 977–80, https://doi.org/10.1080/00131857.2016.1204742; Kathy Hytten, "Deweyan Democracy in a Globalized World," *Educational Theory* 59, no. 4 (2009): 395–408, https://doi.org/10.1111/j.1741-5446.2009.00327.x.

23. https://edtechsummitafrica.org/.

24. Thomas E. Ricks, "Mathematics *Is* Motivating," *The Mathematics Educator* 19, no. 2 (2009/2010): 2–9, https://www.google.com/url?sa=t&rct=j&q=&esrc=s&source=web&cd=2&cad=rja&uact=8&ved=2ahUKEwifu9jOlfvhAhUSZKwKHcELD-kQFjABegQIARAC&url=https%3A%2F%2Ffiles.eric.ed.gov%2Ffulltext%2FEJ882220.pdf.

25. Jonathan Bergmann, and Aaron Sams, *Flipping Learning: Gateway to Student Engagement*, Washington, DC: International Society for Technology Education (ISTE), 2014.

26. Goldberg, 2014

27. Kele Anyanwu, "Teachers Perception in a Technology Integration Workshop: Implications for Professional Development in the Digital Age," *Issues and Trends in Educational Technology* 3, no. 1 (2015): 1–35, https://doi.org/10.2458/azu_itet_v3i1_anyanwu.

28. Fouzieh Sabzian and Abbas Pourhosein Gilakjani, "Teachers' Attitudes about Computer Technology Training, Professional Development, Integration, Experience, Anxiety, and Literacy in English Language Teaching and Learning," *International Journal of Applied Science and Technology* 3, no. 1 (January 2013): 67–75.

29. Mabel Okijie, Anthony A. Olinzock, and Tinuka C. Okojie-Boulder, "The Pedagogy of Technology Integration," *The Journal of Technology Studies* 32, no. 2 (May 2006): 66–71, https://doi.org/10.21061/jots.v32i2.a.1.

30. Anyanwu, "Teachers Perception in a Technology Integration Workshop."

31. Sabzian and Gilakjani, "Teachers' Attitudes about Computer Technology Training."

32. Okijie, Olinzock, and Okojie-Boulder, "The Pedagogy of Technology Integration."

33. Walters and Baffoe-Djan, *What Professional Development*.

34. Matseliso Mokhele & Loyiso C. Jita, "South African Teachers' Perspectives on Continuing Professional Development: A Case Study of the Mpumalanga Secondary Science Initiative," *Procedia Social and Behavioral Sciences* 9, (2010): 1762–66, https://doi.org/10.1016/j.sbspro.2010.12.396; Steyn, "Continuing Professional Development for Teachers in South Africa."

35. Walters and Baffoe-Djan, *What Professional Development*, 2.

36. Mokhele and Jita, "South African Teachers' Perspectives," 1764.

37. Steyn, "Continuing Professional Development for Teachers in South Africa," 28.

38. Ulrich, Jurgens, Ronnie Donaldson, Stephen Rule, and Jürgen Bähr, "Townships in South African Cities–Literature Review and Research Perspectives," *Habitat International* 39, (2013): 256, https://doi.org/10.1016/j.habitatint.2012.10.011.

39. "These are the Biggest Townships in South Africa," Business Tech, August, 14, 2016, https://businesstech.co.za/news/general/132269/these-are-the-biggest-townships-in-south-africa/.

40. William Glasser, *Choice Theory: A New Psychology of Personal Freedom* (New York: Harper Collins, 1999).

41. Diane Heacox, *Differentiating Instruction in the Regular Classroom: How to Reach and Teach All Learners, Grades 3–12* (Minneapolis: Free Spirit Publishers, 2012).

42. English, "John Dewey's Democracy and Education in an Era of Globalization."

43. Maxine Greene, *Releasing the Imagination* (San Francisco: Jossey-Bass, 2000).

44. Bergman and Sams, *Flipping Learning: Gateway to Student Engagement*.

45. Siemens, "Connectivism: A Learning Theory for the Digital Age."

46. Dewey, *Democracy and Education in an Era of Globalization*, 93.

47. John Dewey, *How We Think: A Restatement of the Relation of Reflective Thinking to the Educative Process* (Boston: D.C. Heath and Company Publishers, 1933), 78.

48. Carol Rodgers, "Defining Reflection: Another Look at John Dewey and Reflective Thinking," *Teachers College Record* 104, no. 4 (2002): 845, https://doi.org/10.1111/1467-9620.00181.

49. Bergmann and Sams, *Flipping Learning*.

50. Wenger, *Communities of Practice: Learning, Meaning, and Identity*; Wenger, "Communities of Practice. A Brief Introduction."

51. Glasser, *Choice Theory: A New Psychology of Personal Freedom*.

52. Heacox, *Differentiating Instruction in the Regular Classroom*, 61.

53. Carol Ann Tomlinson, *How to Differentiate Instruction in Mixed Ability Classrooms* (Alexandria: Association for Supervision and Curriculum Development (ASCD), 1995).

54. Christou, "21st-Century Learning," 61.

55. Carol S. Dweck, *Mindset: The New Psychology of Success,* updated edition (New York: Ballantine Books, 2007).

56. Donald A. Schon, *The Reflective Practitioner: How Professionals Think In Action* (San Francisco: Jossey-Bass, 1983); Donald A. Schon, *Educating the Reflective Practitioner: Toward a New Design for Teaching and Learning in the Professions* (San Francisco: Jossey-Bass, 1987).

57. Siemens, "Connectivism: A Learning Theory for the Digital Age."

58. Linda Darling-Hammond, *The Flat World and Education: How America's Commitment to Equity Will Determine Our Future* (New York: Teachers College Press, 2010), 172–73.

59. Sabrina Goldberg, "Energized and Transformed," *EdTech Summit Africa* (Blog), August 18, 2017, https://edtechsummitafrica.tumblr.com/search/Energized%20and%20Transformed%20.

60. Višňovský and Zolcer, "Dewey's Participatory Educational Democracy," 57.

61. Elizabeth Meadows, "Preparing Teachers to Be Curious, Open-Minded, and Actively Reflective: Dewey's Ideas Reconsidered," *Action in Teacher Education* 28, no. 2 (Summer 2006): 4, https://doi.org/10.1080/01626620.2006.10463406.

62. Gordon, "Why Should Scholars Keep Coming Back to John Dewey?" 980.

63. Benson, Puckett, and Harkavay, *Dewey's Dream*, 111.

64. Gordon, "Why Should Scholars Keep Coming Back to John Dewey?"

65. Benson, Puckett, and Harkavay, *Dewey's Dream*.

66. Gordon, "Why Should Scholars Keep Coming Back to John Dewey?" 977.

67. Višňovský and Zolcer, "Dewey's Participatory Educational Democracy," 55.

68. Nebeker, "The Teacher and Society," 19.

69. Meadows, "Preparing Teachers to Be Curious," 4.

70. Ibid., 5–6.

71. Hytten, "Deweyan Democracy in a Globalized World"; Meadows, "Preparing Teachers to Be Curious."

72. Hytten, "Deweyan Democracy in a Globalized World," 395.

73. Ibid., 403.

74. Ibid., 404.

75. Ibid., 405.

76. Ibid.

77. Ibid., 407.

78. Gordon, "Why Should Scholars Keep Coming Back to John Dewey?" 977.

79. English, "John Dewey's Democracy and Education in an Era of Globalization," 1046.

80. Ibid., 1048.

81. Dewey, *Democracy and Education in an Era of Globalization*, 50.

82. John Saltmarsh, Review Essay of *Dewey's Dream: Universities and Democracies in an Age of Education Reform: Civic Society, Public Schools, and Democratic Citizenship* by Lee Benson, Ira Harkavy, and John Puckett, *Michigan Journal of Community Service Learning* 14, no. 1 (2007): 69, http://hdl.handle.net/2027/spo.3239521.0014.106.

83. Hytten, "Deweyan Democracy in a Globalized World."

84. Steyn, "Continuing Professional Development for Teachers in South Africa"; Wenger, "Communities of Practice. A Brief Introduction."

85. Anyanwu, "Teachers Perception in a Technology Integration Workshop"; Mokhele and Jita, "South African Teachers' Perspectives"; Sabzian and Gilakjani, "Teachers' Attitudes about Computer Technology Training."

86. Dewey, *The Public and Its Problems*, 170.

87. Gordon, "Why Should Scholars Keep Coming Back to John Dewey?"; Gordon and English, "John Dewey's Democracy and Education in an Era of Globalization"; English, "John Dewey's Democracy and Education in an Era of Globalization"; Hytten, "Deweyan Democracy in a Globalized World."

88. Dewey, *Democracy and Education,* 100.

89. Amanda Ronan, "Tech Focused Conferences for Educators," Edudemic, December 10, 2015, http://www.edudemic.com/?s=Tech+focused+conferences+for+educators.

90. Steyn, "Continuing Professional Development for Teachers in South Africa"; Wenger, "Communities of Practice. A Brief Introduction."

91. Dewey, *Democracy and Education. An Introduction to the Philosophy of Education* (New York: Macmillan Publishers, 1916), 34.

92. Dewey, *The Public and Its Problems*, 157–58.

93. Ibid., 43.

94. Ibid., 169–70.

95. Ibid., 158.

96. Ghobadi and Ghobadi, "How Access Gaps Interact," 330–40.

97. Ibid., 337.

98. Bornman, "Information Society and Digital Divide in South Africa," 268.

99. Ibid., 268.

100. Mashile, *Technology and the Digital Divide,* 1.

101. Ibid.

102. Benson, Puckett, and Harkavay, *Dewey's Dream*; English, "John Dewey's Democracy and Education in an Era of Globalization"; Višňovský and Zolcer, "Dewey's Participatory Educational Democracy."

103. Gordon, "Why Should Scholars Keep Coming Back to John Dewey?"; Gordon and English, "John Dewey's Democracy and Education in an Era of Globalization"; English, "John Dewey and the Role of the Teacher in a Globalized World"; Hytten, "Deweyan Democracy in a Globalized World."

104. Dewey, *The Public and Its Problems,* 205.

105. Dewey, "Creative Democracy," 4.

106. Ibid., 170.

107. Dewey, *The Public and Its Problems,* 139.

108. Charles Sabel, "Dewey, Democracy and Democratic Experimentalism," *Contemporary Pragmatism* 9, no. 2 (December 2012): 43, https://doi.org/10.1163/18758185-90000229.

109. Bornman, "Information Society and Digital Divide in South Africa," 273.

110. Ibid.

111. Torrey Trust, "Professional Learning Networks Designed for Teacher Learning," *Journal of Digital Learning in Teacher Education* 28, no. 4 (2012): 133–38, https://doi.org/10.1080/21532974.2012.10784693.

112. Ibid., 133.

113. Haythornthwaite and DeLatt, "Social Networks and Learning Networks," 183.

114. Rodgers, 2010, 84

115. Ibid., 89.

116. Ghobadi and Ghobadi, "How Access Gaps Interact," 331.

117. Bornman, "Information Society and Digital Divide in South Africa," 277.

Bibliography

Anyanwu, Kele. "Teachers Perception in a Technology Integration Workshop: Implications for Professional Development in the Digital Age." *Issues and Trends in Educational Technology* 3, no. 1 (2015): 1–35. https://doi.org/10.2458/azu_itet_v3i1_anyanwu.

Benson, Lee, John Puckett, and Ira Harkavay. *Dewey's Dream: Universities and Democracies in an Age of Education Reform, Civil Society, Public Schools, and Democratic Citizenship.* Philadelphia: Temple University Press, 2007.

Bergmann, Jonathan, and Aaron Sams. *Flipping Learning: Gateway to Student Engagement*. Washington, DC: International Society for Technology Education (ISTE), 2014.

Bornman, Elirea. "Information Society and Digital Divide in South Africa: Results of Longitudinal Surveys." *Information, Communication & Society* 19, no. 2 (2016): 264–78. https://doi.org/10.1080/1369118X.2015.1065285.

Christou, Theodore Michael. "21st- Century Learning, Educational Reform, and Tradition: Conceptualizing Professional Development in a Progressive Age." *Teacher Learning and Professional Development* 1, no. 1 (2016): 61–72. http://journals.sfu.ca/tlpd/index.php/tlpd/article/download/10/11.

Cucchiara, Maia. "New Goals, Familiar Challenges? A Brief History of University-Run Schools." In *Perspectives on Urban Education* (Summer 2010): 96–108. https://urbanedjournal.gse.upenn.edu/sites/default/files/pdf_archive/PUE -Summer2010-V7I1-pp96-108.pdf.

Darling-Hammond, Linda. *The Flat World and Education: How America's Commitment to Equity Will Determine Our Future*. New York: Teachers College Press, 2010.

De Latt, Maarten. *Enabling Professional Development Networks: How Connected Are You?* Heerlen: Open University, 2012.

Dewey, John. (1940). Creative Democracy. The task before us: 1-4. http://www .beloit.edu/~pbk/dewey.html

———. *Democracy and Education. An Introduction to the Philosophy of Education*. New York: Macmillan Publishers, 1916.

———. *How We Think: A Restatement of the Relation of Reflective Thinking to the Educative Process*. Boston: D.C. Heath and Company Publishers, 1933; New York: Dover Publications, 2012.

———. (1927) 2016. *The Public and Its Problems: An Essay in Political Inquiry*, edited by Melvin L. Rogers. Athens: Ohio University Press.

———. *Experience and Education*, The Kappa Delta Pi Lecture Series. New York: Free Press, 2015.

Dweck, Carol S. *Mindset: The New Psychology of Success*, updated edition. New York: Ballantine Books, 2007.

English, Andrea R. "John Dewey and the Role of the Teacher in a Globalized World: Imagination, Empathy, and 'Third Voice.'" *Educational Philosophy and Theory* 48, no. 10 (2016): 1046–64. https://doi.org/10.1080/00131857.2016.1202806.

Ghobadi, Shahla, and Zahra Ghobadi. "How Access Gaps Interact and Shape the Digital Divide: A Cognitive Investigation." *Behaviour & Information Technology* 34, no. 4 (2015): 330–40. http://dx.doi.org/10.1080/014492 9X.2013.833650.

Glasser, William. *Choice Theory: A New Psychology of Personal Freedom*. New York: Harper Collins, 1999.

Goldberg, Sabrina. "Energized and Transformed." *EdTech Summit Africa* (Blog), August 18, 2017. https://edtechsummitafrica.tumblr.com/search/Energized%20 and%20Transformed%20.

———. The Great Mathematician Project. *Mathematics Teaching in the Middle School* 19, no. 5 (2013/2014), 272–79.

Gordon, Mordecai. "Why Should Scholars Keep Coming Back to John Dewey?" *Journal of Educational Philosophy* 48, no. 10 (2016): 1077–91. https://doi.org /10.1080/00131857.2016.1150800.

Gordon, Mordecai and Andrea R. English. "John Dewey's Democracy and Education in an Era of Globalization." *Educational Philosophy* 48, no. 10 (2016): 977–80. https://doi.org/10.1080/00131857.2016.1204742.

Greene, Maxine. *Releasing the Imagination*. San Francisco: Jossey-Bass, 2000.

Haythornthwaite, Caroline, and Maarten DeLatt. "Social Networks and Learning Networks: Using Social Network Perspectives to Understand Learning." In *Proceedings of the 7th International Conference on Networked Learning*, edited by Lone Dirckinck-Holmfeld, Vivien Hodgson, Chris Jones, Maarten de Laat, David McConnell, and Thomas Ryberg, 183–90. Lancaster: Lancaster University, 2010. https://www.lancaster.ac.uk/fss/organisations/netlc/past /nlc2010/abstracts/PDFs/Haythornwaite.pdf.

Heacox, Diane. *Differentiating Instruction in the Regular Classroom: How to Reach and Teach All Learners, Grades 3–12*. Minneapolis: Free Spirit Publishers, 2012.

Henning, Elizabeth, Gadija Petker, and Nadine Petersen. "University-Affiliated Schools as Sites for Research Learning in Pre-Service Teacher Education." *South African Journal of Education* 35, no. 1 (2015): 1–8. https://doi.org /10.15700/201503070014.

Hytten, Kathy. "Deweyan Democracy in a Globalized World." *Educational Theory* 59, no. 4 (2009): 395–408. https://doi.org/10.1111/j.1741-5446.2009.00327.x.

Jurgens, Ulrich, Ronnie Donaldson, Stephen Rule, and Jürgen Bähr. "Townships in South African Cities – Literature Review and Research Perspectives." *Habitat International* 39, (2013): 256–60. https://doi.org/10.1016/j.habitatint .2012.10.011.

Mashile, Thubelihlelenkululeko Zonke. *Technology and the Digital Divide: Understanding Factors that Impact on Educators' Ability to Integrate Technology in South African Classrooms*. Illovo: Gordon Institute of Business Science, University of Pretoria, 2016.

Meadows, Elizabeth. "Preparing Teachers to Be Curious, Open-Minded, and Actively Reflective: Dewey's Ideas Reconsidered." *Action in Teacher Education* 28, no. 2 (Summer 2006): 4–14. https://doi.org/10.1080/01626620.2006.1046 3406.

Mokhele, Matseliso, and Loyiso C. Jita. "South African Teachers' Perspectives on Continuing Professional Development: A Case Study of the Mpumalanga

Secondary Science Initiative." *Procedia Social and Behavioral Sciences* 9, (2010): 1762–66. https://doi.org/10.1016/j.sbspro.2010.12.396.

Nebeker, Melia L. "The Teacher and Society: John Dewey and the Experience of Teachers." *Education and Culture* XIX, no. 2 (Fall 2002):14–20. https://www.jstor.org/stable/42922389.

November, Alan. *Empowering Students with Technology,* 2nd ed. Thousand Oaks: Corwin Press, 2009.

Okijie, Mabel, Anthony A. Olinzock, and Tinuka C. Okojie-Boulder. "The Pedagogy of Technology Integration." *The Journal of Technology Studies* 32, no. 2 (May 2006): 66–71. https://doi.org/10.21061/jots.v32i2.a.1.

Rachmajanti, Sri and Maureen McClure. "University-Affiliated Lab Schools: A Collaborative Partnership Between the University of Pittsburgh's Falk School, and the State University of Malang Lab Schools." *Excellence in Higher Education* 2, no. 1 (2011): 11–20. https://doi.org/10.5195/ehe.2011.40.

Ricks, Thomas E. "Mathematics *Is* Motivating." *The Mathematics Educator* 19, no. 2 (2009/2010): 2–9. https://www.google.com/url?sa=t&rct=j&q=&esrc=s&source=web&cd=2&cad=rja&uact=8&ved=2ahUKEwifu9jOlfvhAhUSZKwKHcELD-kQFjABegQIARAC&url=https%3A%2F%2Ffiles.eric.ed.gov%2Ffulltext%2FEJ882220.pdf.

Rodgers, Carol. "Defining Reflection: Another Look at John Dewey and Reflective Thinking." *Teachers College Record* 104, no. 4 (2002): 842–66. https://doi.org/10.1111/1467-9620.00181.

Ronan, Amanda. "Tech Focused Conferences for Educators." Edudemic, December 10, 2015. http://www.edudemic.com/?s=Tech+focused+conferences+for+educators.

Sabel, Charles. "Dewey, Democracy and Democratic Experimentalism." *Contemporary Pragmatism* 9, no. 2 (December 2012): 35–55. https://doi.org/10.1163/18758185-90000229.

Sabzian, Fouzieh, and Abbas Pourhosein Gilakjani. "Teachers' Attitudes about Computer Technology Training, Professional Development, Integration, Experience, Anxiety, and Literacy in English Language Teaching and Learning." *International Journal of Applied Science and Technology* 3, no. 1 (January 2013): 67–75.

Saltmarsh, John. Review Essay of *Dewey's Dream: Universities and Democracies in an Age of Education Reform: Civic Society, Public Schools, and Democratic Citizenship* by Lee Benson, Ira Harkavy, and John Puckett. *Michigan Journal of Community Service Learning* 14, no. 1 (2007): 65–77. http://hdl.handle.net/2027/spo.3239521.0014.106.

Schon, Donald A. *The Reflective Practitioner: How Professionals Think In Action.* San Francisco: Jossey-Bass, 1983.

———. *Educating the Reflective Practitioner: Toward a New Design for Teaching and Learning in the Professions.* San Francisco: Jossey-Bass, 1987.

Siemens, G. "Connectivism: A learning theory for the digital age." *International Journal of Instructional Technology and Distance Learning* 2, no. 1 (2005). http://itdl.org/journal/jan_05/article01.htm.

Sparks, Sarah D. "Amid Changing Landscapes, Lab Schools Search for New Roles." In *Education Week*, February 24, 2015. https://www.edweek.org/ew/articles/2015/02/25/lab-schools-search-for-new-roles.html.

Steyn, G. M. "Continuing Professional Development for Teachers in South Africa and Social Learning Systems: Conflicting Conceptual Frameworks of Learning." *Koers* 73, no. 1 (July 2008): 15–31. https://doi.org/10.4102/koers.v73i1.151.

"These are the Biggest Townships in South Africa." *Business Tech.* August 14, 2016. https://businesstech.co.za/news/general/132269/these-are-the-biggest-townships-in-south-africa/.

Tomlinson, Carol Ann. *How to Differentiate Instruction in Mixed Ability Classrooms.* Alexandria: Association for Supervision and Curriculum Development (ASCD), 1995.

Trust, Torrey. "Professional Learning Networks Designed for Teacher Learning." *Journal of Digital Learning in Teacher Education* 28, no. 4 (2012): 133–38. https://doi.org/10.1080/21532974.2012.10784693.

Višňovský, Emil, and Štefan Zolcer. "Dewey's Participatory Educational Democracy." *Educational Theory* 66, no. 1–2 (2016): 55–71. https://doi.org/10.1111/edth.12152.

Walters, Catherine, and Jessica Briggs Baffoe-Djan. *What Professional Development Makes the Most Difference to Teachers?* Oxford: Oxford University Press, 2012.

Wenger, Etienne. *Communities of Practice: Learning, Meaning, and Identity.* Cambridge: Cambridge University Press, 1998. http://dx.doi.org/10.1017/CBO9780511803932.

———. "Communities of Practice. A Brief Introduction." Paper presented at the STEP Leadership Workshop, University of Oregon, OR, October 2011. https://scholarsbank.uoregon.edu/xmlui/bitstream/handle/1794/11736/A%20brief%20introduction%20to%20CoP.pdf?sequence=1&isAllowed=y.

Sabrina R. Goldberg, Ed.D., is the lead 7th grade mathematics teacher at The School at Columbia University.

JOHN DEWEY, AMERICA'S PEACE-MINDED EDUCATOR

Catherine Colagross Willoughby

Charles F. Howlett and Audrey Cohan, *John Dewey, America's Peace-Minded Educator*. Carbondale: Southern Illinois University Press, 2016. 307 pp. ISBN 978-0-809-33504-6. $50.46 (pbk).

After reading *John Dewey, America's Peace-Minded Educator*, written by Charles F. Howlett and Audrey Cohan, it would be easy to see how contemporary issues such as the call for a national border wall and the characterization of immigrants as a threat to national security would have incensed John Dewey if he were still alive. Dewey, as depicted by Howlett and Cohan, was an educator who believed that democracy should be shared and preserved in a peaceful manner if it were to be achieved. "Peace-minded" Dewey would have encouraged "teaching the immigrant population about adjustment and improvement in American society" (28). He would have encouraged Americans to embrace and work at understanding immigrants, not shut them out. He believed that world peace needed to be achieved through workable means. Through his published writings, personal letters, and books written by other authors, Howlett and Cohan uncover Dewey's views on peace and organize it chronologically, beginning with the trauma he remembers as a child during the Civil War (16). Though he wavered on how to achieve peace (which caused him to be scrutinized and misunderstood by people at times), he never wavered on his desire for peace. His encouragement of the idea of "creating of a Great Community on a global scale" is why Howlett and Cohan argue that he "still deserves our attention today" (239).

In the first chapter, Howlett and Cohan assert that Dewey formed his ideas on peace at a very young age. He was only five when he was uprooted from his home to be closer to his father, who was captain of the Union volunteers during the Civil War. He rarely saw his father, and the "devastation and carnage caused by the conflict left a deep impression on him and his brothers" (16). This impression carried into his adult life: "Certainly the disruption of family life and the social and economic dislocations cause by the war influenced Dewey's later thinking about reform issues" (18). As industries began to grow in the post-Civil War era, there was unrest among large groups of workers due to poor working conditions. As a young professor at the University of Michigan, he began to "witness the beginnings of violence stemming from social discontent" (19) and ten years later he joined the faculty at the University of Chicago, where the authors note that he began to be viewed as a "social critic" (24). In Chicago, he was able to be closer to reformers like Jane Addams, who cofounded Hull House with Ellen Gates Starr, to promote pragmatic peaceful projects that helped to "bridge class cultures" and push for "factory legislation and better city services" (26). His connection with like-minded people fueled his idea that education should teach social morality and enable "children to see life as it really was" (33). In his mind this was necessary for establishing useful social relationships that could minimize conflict among workers and immigrants by uplifting them, thus encouraging peaceful relationships.

In Chapter 2, Howlett and Cohan argue that Dewey altered his position on peace, which drew criticism from some of his contemporaries, as conflict among nations began brewing before the start of World War I. They explain how Dewey began espousing the belief that war was necessary to ensure the spread of democracy and that it would not be possible for peace to be achieved by passively wishing for it. He joined other social critics arguing that this war needed to be fought for the greater good and to further ideas of social reform and democracy. Dewey also argued that an Allied victory "in turn might guarantee and ensure the creation of a new world order based on peace and democracy" (46), and that if "government agencies could effectively organize a nation for war, they could also work to upgrade the standard of living by fighting a war against industrial abuse and capitalistic oppression" (49). He continued this stance until the end of the war. Dewey's robust enthusiasm for war as an agent of change then soured when the treaty of Versailles was signed. Its harsh treatment of Germany disillusioned him: "[h]e now reasoned that the war had failed to bring about both a regeneration of the nation and a lasting advance toward international peace" (69). After the war, *active* postwar peace organizations began to form, and Howlett and Cohan observe that Dewey joined the movement, altering his previous stance on war because it fit with his view that peace needed to be functional to be successful.

In the middle of the book (chapters 3–5), Howlett and Cohan show evidence that Dewey became disillusioned by the way people in the United States and other countries promulgated the peace movement, though it remained an important issue to him. Even though there were peace talks in Paris at the end of World War I, the victors did not treat the defeated kindly; they were very punitive toward Germany. As he was lecturing in the Far East, Dewey noticed that the Japanese behaved the same way toward the Chinese as the French did toward the Germans. Both the French and the Japanese exploited resources from the Germans and the Chinese, respectively. Without US intervention, he feared that China's open-door policy would make room for Japan to exercise its "imperialistic ambitions" (90).

During his time in the Far East, and when he returned home, pacifist groups in the United States were attending peace conferences and creating organizations to counteract the perception that the United States was starting to become too peaceful and complacent (98). In order to "promote the message of world peace and democratic justice" (98), Dewey began to spread his message to secondary schools and colleges, where military training had infiltrated, He was strongly against the promotion of military training in secondary schools and colleges. As Howlett and Cohan argue, "If there was one consistent and unbending policy that Dewey adhered to throughout his entire life, it was his opposition to any form of military training in an academic environment" (99). The mechanical, noncognitve aspects of military training were the "antithesis of his pedagogy" (100). He believed they would promote "a system that [would] lead only to unquestioned obedience to the state and those positions of authority" (101). This conviction led Dewey to devote much of his postwar time supporting the Outlawry of War crusade, a movement to "outlaw war as a legal method of settling disputes" (125). Though it was supported by the government (Paris Pact), it was never really taken seriously. The movement lacked the support and convictions of those in power necessary to enforce it.

At the end of the book (chapters 6 and 7), the United States begins to slide toward World War II, and Howlett and Cohan write that Dewey was opposed to the prospect of war for its devastating effects on international peace and its likely "impact . . . on civil liberties at home" (202). He was troubled by the way Americans who were against the war were treated and how Japanese Americans were targeted, even though there was no proof that they were a threat to the United States: "the displacement experience of Japanese Americans and the herding of hundreds of conscientious objectors into public service camps characterized by strict regimentation and unconscionable medical experimentation were a constant reminder to him that the insidious aspects of ultranationalism sweeping the country posed a serious threat to the preservation of civil liberties" (216). Dewey spent his time during and after the war as an activist for the preservation of these liberties. Even after the war, Howlett and Cohan point out that Dewey never gave up on the idea that "intelligence would one day solve the problem of war" (218). He believed this until the day he died.

In thoughtfully sifting and sorting his published writings, personal letters, and books written by other authors, Howlett and Cohan have written a book that really showcases Dewey as a "peace-minded" educator. Though he was criticized by his contemporaries for wavering on *how* peace should be achieved, he never stopped thinking that it *could* be achieved. He believed that peace could be attained if people established useful social relationships and worked for their mutual uplift. He believed that social morality should be taught in schools so that children would be ready to face the world as global citizens. Never have Dewey's words seemed as relevant as they are today. In a country where we are contemplating building a wall to separate ourselves from others, Dewey's peace-minded views could offer a different way to look at the issue of border security.

Catherine Colagross Willoughby, Ph.D., is an adjunct professor at Oakland University and the University of West Florida, and has over twenty years of experience in the field of education. She has created online courses for institutions including Michigan Virtual University and Central Michigan University. Currently, she teaches online and hybrid courses to graduate students and studies the impact of e-learning on K–12 and higher education.

Comparative Assessment in John Dewey, Confucius, and Global Philosophy

Holly Walker-Coté

Introduction

Joseph Grange's book, *John Dewey, Confucius, and Global Philosophy*, seeks to create a dialogue between Dewey's pragmatism and Confucianism in order to analyze the two traditions and parse out their more salient, and similar, tenets. In order to provide a comparative analysis of Eastern and Western traditions, it is necessary to establish a starting point since they are inherently different due to the cultures in which they have traditionally been embedded.

Grange references the popular comparison of John Dewey to a "Second Confucius" and sets out to make a case for this comparison. Grange offers a comparative look at the philosophical underpinnings of Confucianism and the ways in which its more salient points can be interwoven with Dewey's thinking. Grange's goal is to weave together a tapestry that includes, in as equal measures as possible, the more salient points of Dewey's and Confucius's ways of seeing the world and how those worldviews can open up a new dialogue regarding the ultimate good for society.

Summary

Grange takes an economical approach to the book, acknowledging that the best route to saliency is trimming the fat from what could otherwise be a cumbersome topic. The study focuses on three main thematic points: experience, felt intelligence, and culture. Grange approaches his comparative exercise by introducing Dewey's main ideas and then responding to them by presenting similar Confucian principles. By parsing out paired themes in the two philosophies, Grange illustrates similarities and creates a dialogue between the two. Grange tells us that his "aim is to present these interwoven themes as a support system for a cross-cultural dialogue on global understanding" (xv). It is Grange's position that Western philosophy's systematic nature can be balanced out (yin and yang) by Chinese philosophy's demands for binary solutions.

In addressing the theme of experience, Grange explains that Dewey used the term "experience" for its broad meaning in order to indicate the vast possibilities that can be observed within humanity. What we experience can be expressed in the physical, psychological, and spiritual realms. The Confucian equivalent to experience is the Dao, or the Way, on which Confucian philosophy and its path for living are based. Grange describes experience as an event rather than a thing. Experience is what occurs within the context of other experiences and creates a ripple effect that, in turn, stimulates experience for others. Experience happens on the individual level, but all things are interdependent as well, so experience can evidence varying degrees of complexity. When new experience occurs, the newness of it forces growth and, thus, transformation. Our connection to the world is dependent upon our social conditioning, the environment in which the experience takes place, and the ways in which we bump into each other as these things occur. In Dewey's view, we are constantly engaged in experience and subjected to it, making us actors and reactors at the same time. Our best bet for harmony between the acting and reacting is to arrive at a level of experience whereby we have acquired the ability to gain perspective, and with perspective, the ability to reason out purpose from experience and seek further growth.

Dewey divides experience into two categories: instrumental and consummatory. Instrumental experience refers to the subject matter of each experience we will encounter, while consummatory experience refers to the deep values we feel through experience. The example that Grange offers is that of a piece of art and the artist's ability to take everyday objects that are recognizable (paint, paper, etc.) and transform them into a new object with variety and novelty: "A genuine consummatory experience dissolves separations and heals the splits in culture" (12).

Grange begins his contrast to Dewey's concept of experience by discussing the Dao (the Way) and the fact that the Way is created by the person who experiences it. In order to engage one's self with the Way, one must be engaged in the "matter at hand," which falls under Dewey's category of the instrumental experience. Second, Grange cites the concept of "de" as an idea within the Dao that seeks excellence. The "de" can be seen also as the inherent truth of any experience and, therefore, a desirable consequence of engaging in the Way. Third, Grange directs us to the concept of "Ren," which he interprets as "humanity," and which he indicates is the most important commonality between Dewey's philosophy and Confucianism. "Ren" anticipates growth and expansion; that is, the hope of growing in the Way as Dewey would hope for growth in experience.

In his discussion of the "split" or division that causes tension in our culture, Grange reaches back to the Cartesian Paradigm to argue that the divide between the mind and the body is the source of our problematic relationship with experience. On one hand, we feel the world in our experience, and on the other, we reason our way through it by interpreting our experience intellectually. Dewey's idea of experience as the conduit of knowledge was a way to join the body and mind together, and heal the fissure between these two modalities of interpreting reality. Grange uses the Confucian concept of "li" to compare with the idea of felt intelligence. In Confucianism, "li" refers to the observance of ritual, which, in Dewey's mode of thinking, would compare to the contact with others in the social sphere that creates meaning within the community.

Grange's book offers an easily digestible analysis of Dewey's main tenets and how they support and feed into each other to reinforce his worldview. Grange makes sure to place Dewey in his historical and social context, as well as within the context of his philosophical lineage, so the reader understands the continuity of his work as it related to his predecessors. The author provides insights on the more complicated of the topics within Dewey's pragmatism, perhaps a result of years of teaching and having dialogue with students. Unfortunately, where the work falls short is in the contextualization of Confucianism in Chinese culture and history. Early on, Grange states that his goal for the book is to weave together the two philosophies in order to create a path to a better world. In the end, there is not enough to stitch together between Dewey and Confucius to link the "low-context" American culture of thought to the "high-context" Chinese culture of thought. While not without merits, and while there are certainly similarities to be studied and connections to be made, it seems that the goal of the book is really to make a case for the idiomatic phrase that Dewey was a "Second Confucius" rather than to deconstruct the Second Confucianism of John Dewey and how that could come to pass.

Overall, Grange's book offers an in-depth look at John Dewey's contribution to pragmatism and the inner workings of his approach to finding continuity between the parts of the whole. This book would be helpful for those who are interested in understanding Dewey's discussion of experience and the various manifestations of experience as a foundation of human existence within the realms of the mind, body, and society. Grange's comparative discussion utilizing Confucianism allows us to take some of Dewey's ideas and apply them to another context in order to shake out differences and similarities between the cultures and habits of thinking. While perhaps not a useful introduction to Confucianism per se, there are some items to be learned about the foundations of Chinese philosophy and the bedrock upon which it is built. Grange has taken complex matter and parsed it out in a way that is very accessible to the reader and will offer a very comprehensible look into Dewey's basic philosophical principles.

ABOUT THE AUTHOR

Joseph Grange was a pragmatist and philosophy professor at the University of Southern Maine. Before his death in 2014, he had served as the president of the Metaphysical Society of America as well as director of the Society for the Study of Process Philosophies. Grange based his academic lectures on his reflections on

Plato's Idea of The Good as the foundation of being and knowledge. Grange had a deep interest in comparative philosophy after spending time both in China and teaching for three years in Hawaii, during which time he studied Chinese philosophy under C. Y. Cheng and Roger Ames. This, his final book, is the culmination of his academic studies and attempt to make sense of the similarities and differences between the Eastern and Western traditions that held his interest.

BIBLIOGRAPHY

Grange, Joseph. *John Dewey, Confucius, and Global Philosophy.* New York: State University of New York Press, 2004.

Holly Walker-Coté is a lecturer of Spanish language and culture and a doctoral student in educational leadership at Oakland University in Rochester, Michigan.